Titanic

Titanic

Freak Accident or Farce?

Andrew Norman

First published in Great Britain in 2025 by
Pen & Sword History
An imprint of Pen & Sword Books Limited
Yorkshire – Philadelphia

Copyright © Andrew Norman 2025

ISBN 978 1 03610 016 2

The right of Andrew Norman to be identified as
Author of this Work has been asserted by him in accordance
with the Copyright, Designs and Patents Act 1988.

A CIP catalogue record for this book is
available from the British Library.

All rights reserved. No part of this book may be reproduced, transmitted, downloaded, decompiled or reverse engineered in any form or by any means, electronic or mechanical, including photocopying, recording or by any information storage and retrieval system, without permission from the Publisher in writing. NO AI TRAINING: Without in any way limiting the Author's and Publisher's exclusive rights under copyright, any use of this publication to 'train' generative artificial intelligence (AI) technologies to generate text is expressly prohibited. The Author and Publisher reserve all rights to license uses of this work for generative AI training and development of machine learning language models.

Typeset by Mac Style
Printed in the UK by CPI Group (UK) Ltd, Croydon, CR0 4YY.

The Publisher's authorised representative in the EU for product safety is Authorised Rep Compliance Ltd., Ground Floor, 71 Lower Baggot Street, Dublin D02 P593, Ireland.
www.arccompliance.com

For a complete list of Pen & Sword titles please contact:

PEN & SWORD BOOKS LIMITED
47 Church Street, Barnsley, South Yorkshire, S70 2AS, England
E-mail: enquiries@pen-and-sword.co.uk
Website: www.pen-and-sword.co.uk
or
PEN AND SWORD BOOKS
1950 Lawrence Road, Havertown, PA 19083, USA
E-mail: uspen-and-sword@casematepublishers.com
Website: www.penandswordbooks.com

Contents

Acknowledgements		viii
Author's Note		ix
A Question of Time?		x

Part I: Hubris   1

1	*Titanic*: The World's Largest Movable Object: The White Star Line	3
2	*Titanic*: A Further Description	5
3	*Titanic's* Decks	9
4	Lifeboats and Safety Equipment	14
5	First Class Luxury!	17
6	*Titanic* Sets Sail	19
7	*Titanic's* Captain, Edward Smith	22
8	Captain Smith: Bravado: Previous Mishaps	26
9	*Titanic's* Officers	29
10	*Titanic's* Crew	33
11	*Titanic's* Passengers	39
12	Safety: The Board of Trade Passenger Certificate: Failure to Perform a Lifeboat Drill	41
13	The Atlantic Ocean Beckons: 'Tracks'	43
14	The Weather and Sea Conditions up to the Night of 14/15 April 1912	46

15	Sunday 14 April 1912: Captain Smith's Instructions to his Officers and Their Instructions to *Titanic*'s Lookouts: What They Saw	49
16	*Titanic*'s Lookouts: Their Previous Experience and Capabilities	51
17	The Mystery of the Missing Binoculars	54
18	Warnings of Ice and Icebergs, Some of Which Did Not Reach the Bridge, and All of Which Captain Smith Chose to Ignore	57
19	Aboard *Titanic*, was there any Inkling of Ice of Icebergs in the Vicinity?	63
20	Who was On Watch on that Fateful Night of 14/15 April 1912? First Sight of the Iceberg	64

Part II: Nemesis — 67

21	The Collision: The Fatal Turn to Port	69
22	The Outcome of the Impact	76
23	Survival! The Inadequately Filled Lifeboats	79
24	The Ice Field into which *Titanic* had Sailed	84
25	The Speed of *Titanic* on Impact with the Iceberg: Visibility at the Crucial Time: Time Available to React to the Presence of the Iceberg	88
26	The Origin of Icebergs: Were Icebergs a One-off Phenomenon in 1912, at the Location in the Atlantic Ocean where *Titanic* Sank?	95
27	The Invidious Position of *Titanic*'s Lookouts: Absence of Searchlights; Absence of Binoculars; Absence of Goggles	97
28	Fate of the Captain, Passengers and Crew: Human Drama and Human Tragedy	100

29	The Alleged Negligence of Captain Stanley Lord of the SS *Californian*	105
30	Captain Lord's Defence	110
31	Captains Smith and Lord Compared	116
32	Second Officer Lightoller's Account in More Detail	118
33	Weaknesses in *Titanic*'s Design and Construction	125
34	Verdict of the UK and US Inquiries	128
35	J. Bruce Ismay's Testimony to the UK and US Inquiries	131
36	Morgan Robertson's Prophetic Novella: The Wreck of the Titan Or, *Futility* (1898): What If?	139
37	Eva Hart: A Survivor's Account	143
38	Bernice Palmer, Her Camera, and the Iceberg	146
39	An Eminently Avoidable Accident: The Assumption that *Titanic* was Unsinkable	148
40	The Debt Owed to Guglielmo Marconi	149
41	The 1997 Dive on *Titanic*	153
42	Captain Smith: A Classic and Tragic Case of 'Hubris Syndrome'	157

Appendix: Provisions	161
Notes	162
Bibliography	173
Index	174

Acknowledgements

Jean M. Bennett; Bernard C. Burgess; Hester Cribb, Jan Marsh, Poole Maritime Trust, Poole, Dorset, UK; Randall A. Rosenfeld, Archivist, Royal Astronomical Society of Canada.

Photographs were obtained from *Wikimedia Commons* unless otherwise stated.

Author's Note

There has been speculation over the loss of the Royal Mail Ship (RMS) *Titanic* ever since the tragic event of her sinking occurred during the night of Sunday 14 to Monday 15 April 1912. Is it possible to be certain of *anything* in respect of *Titanic*? Certainly. Records are available in regard to her physical dimensions, layout of decks, fuel consumption, provisions carried, number of passengers and crew, number of lifeboats, etcetera, on her final fateful journey. However, what is less certain concerns the events which took place prior to her sinking.

What is to be relied upon in this respect? Fortunately, the accounts of eyewitnesses are contained in the two subsequent enquiries which took place shortly afterwards, one in the USA and the other in the UK. The problem is, however, that eyewitness accounts are not always reliable, and two people may differ in their recollections of the same event. Therefore, any conclusion in respect of the loss of *Titanic* must be based on a balance of probability, in the same way that a jury, having assessed the evidence in a criminal trial, has to make the decision whether 'guilty', 'not guilty', or 'not proven, Your Honour'. In short, what it boils down to is, what may be concluded from the body of evidence, and can this evidence be trusted?

I studied physics at Oxford, which is useful when it comes to understanding, for instance, how starlight reflects off an iceberg. I also studied physiology, during which time I took part in an experiment to see how long a person can survive in water at low temperatures – viz. those from the *Titanic* who found themselves struggling in the freezing cold sea. The answer? Some 15 to 45 minutes, or possibly up to one hour with protective clothing.

I also studied psychology and psychiatry, which had proved invaluable when attempting to fathom the mindset of *Titanic*'s captain, Edward John Smith.

As a young teenager I lived at the Beacon School, Lichfield, Staffordshire, of which my father was headmaster. This was within a mile of Beacon Park, where there was a statue of Commander Edward J. Smith by British sculptor

Kathleen Scott. The statue was unveiled on 29 July 1914 in the presence of the captain's widow, Eleanor, and his daughter, Helen. Six days later on 4 August 1914, the First World War commenced. Of course, I had no idea if the significance of this at the time, nor of the fact that one day I would write a book about the *Titanic*!

Smith was born in Hanley, Staffordshire on 27 January 1850 and on 15 April 2012, a plaque in his honour was unveiled in Hanley Town Hall to mark the centenary of *Titanic*'s sinking.

By another coincidence, my present home at Poole, in South Dorset, is within a short distance of the Haven Hotel at Sandbanks, Poole, Dorset in Southern England, where Italian inventor Guglielmo Marconi lived for a time and conducted his early experiments in wireless telegraphy. It is thanks to Marconi that those who survived the sinking of *Titanic* were able to be rescued, for without his invention of the Marconigram wireless telegraph, which was fitted to all the ships involved including *Titanic*, *all the passengers and crew would have drowned.*

At Studland, which is also not far from my home, lived Jacob W. Gibbons, steward aboard *Titanic*, who survived and wrote poignantly about the tragedy.

A near neighbour of mine here in Poole, Dorset is Mrs Hester Cribb, whose late husband John Hatfield Cribb was the grandson and namesake of John Hatfield Cribb, who sailed aboard the *Titanic* with his 17-year-old daughter Laura May Cribb, whose occupation was shop assistant.

John senior, who was born in Australia, married Bessie Jane Welch of Parkstone, Poole, and the family lived for a while in Newark, New Jersey, USA where John worked as Assistant Steward at the Essex Club. However, the family returned to the UK and in 1911 were living in Salterns Road, Poole.

Laura and her father John sailed aboard *Titanic* as third-class passengers, destined for Newark, New Jersey, it being the intention that the rest of the family should join them and settle there permanently.

In her account entitled 'My Experience on the RMS *Titanic*', Laura described how, on the evening of Sunday 15 April she went to bed at 10:50 pm and was 'soon fast asleep'. Having woken up and been awake for 'quite three minutes', she said, 'suddenly the ship trembled violently, then stopped with a jerk'. Soon after, 'the Captain and Officers came hurrying along and shouting as loudly as they could: 'Gentlemen, assist the women and children to get their lifebelts on, then go up on deck all of you'. Hester believes, however, that Laura wrote an earlier account, critical of the White Star Line, which has not survived. This, she thinks, is because the company threatened punitive action against anyone who acted in this manner.

The last Laura saw of her father was when she was getting into the third Lifeboat the crew of which had difficulty in rowing away from *Titanic* as the suction was 'so very strong'. Laura then witnessed 'a terrific thunderous explosion, followed by the most terrible shrieks and groans of the helpless and doomed people that were left on the wreck of the great ship, the explosion having caused the ship to split in half, and then it sank very rapidly indeed'.

By the time Laura's lifeboat reached the *Carpathia*, her body was 'so stiff with the intense cold', she said, 'that I could not climb the rope ladder' which had been let down over the side, 'so I had to have the belt and rope adjusted under my arms and round my waist'. This was in order for her to be hoisted aboard.

Finally, Laura returned to the UK aboard the SS *Celtic*, to be reunited with her mother and younger siblings, Ernest, Ellen, and Frank.

On 12 November 1916, in Poole, Laura married engineer and mechanic Howard Marsh Buzzell of Carlsbad, New Mexico, USA. They had met in October 1916 whilst passengers aboard the RMS *Baltic*, bound for Liverpool from the USA. The couple had five children.

No one has hitherto managed to explain Captain Smith's mindset, and thereby comprehend why, on a dark night in April 1912, he drove his ship full tilt into an ice field when he knew that there were icebergs present. Was the captain mentally ill? No, not in the sense of having one of the traditional major psychiatric conditions such as schizophrenia, psychosis, bipolar disorder, etcetera, because this would have manifested itself earlier on in his lifetime. In fact, Captain Smith's state of mind provides a classic example of what was described by the ancient Greeks more than 2,000 years ago!

A Question of Time?

In the early twentieth century, time zones as we know them today did not exist. Instead, on ocean liners and on other ships, clocks were adjusted daily so that they read 12:00 when the sun was at its highest point in the sky. (This was known as Local Apparent Noon, 'LAN'. For example, on Sunday 14 April 1912, the day when *Titanic* struck the iceberg at 12.40 p.m., her clocks were running at 2 hours and 2 minutes ahead of New York Time, and 2 hours and 58 minutes behind Greenwich Mean Time.

This had the advantage that for passengers and crew, daytime and nighttime were similar to when they were on land. It also meant that before arrival is a distant port, especially if many lines of longitude had been crossed, only a small time adjustment was necessary.

For the purpose of this narrative, the time to which the clocks were set aboard *Titanic* at the various stages of her voyage (ship's time or bridge time) will be referred to as '*Titanic* Time', or by the acronym 'TT'.

Part I
Hubris

1

Titanic: The World's Largest Movable Object: The White Star Line

RMS (Royal Mail Ship) *Titanic* was one of three Olympic Class liners, the other two being RMS Britannic (which was sunk by a mine during the First World War) and RMS *Olympic*.

Olympic and *Titanic* were sister ships, built at the Harland & Wolff shipyard, Belfast for the White Star Line. Both Sir Edward J. Harland and Gustav W. Wolff were shipbuilders and politicians, Harland being British and Wolff being German.

The first company to bear the name 'White Star Line' was founded in Liverpool, England, by John Pilkington and Henry Wilson in 1845. 'It focused on the UK–Australia trade, which increased following the discovery of gold in Australia in 1851'.

On 18 January 1868, the White Star Line having failed, Liverpool shipowner Thomas Ismay 'purchased the house flag, trade name and goodwill of the bankrupt company for £1,000, with the intention of operating large steamships on the North Atlantic service between Liverpool and New York'. Accordingly, Ismay established the company's headquarters at Albion House, Liverpool. When Gustav Christian Schwabe, a prominent Liverpool merchant, and his nephew, the shipbuilder Gustav Wilhelm Wolff, 'offered to finance the new line if Ismay had his ships built by Wolff's company, Harland and Wolff, Ismay agreed, and a partnership with Harland and Wolff was established'. In 1870, Liverpool shipowner William Imrie joined the managing company.[1]

Chief Designer of both *Olympic* and *Titanic* was 57-year-old Ulsterman Alexander M. Carlisle, brother-in-law of Lord Pirrie, Chairman of the White Star Line and director of Harland & Wolff.

On the death of his father Thomas on 23 November 1899, J. Bruce Ismay, became Chairman of the White Star Line and its Managing Director.

4   Titanic

Prior to 1907, the White Star Line's main transatlantic service ran from Liverpool via Queenstown in southern Ireland to New York. However, in that year the company transferred its transatlantic headquarters from Liverpool to Southampton. The main transatlantic service now ran from Southampton, via Cherbourg in northern France and Queenstown, to New York. At Southampton new docks were built by the White Star Company in order to accommodate its huge new *Olympic* class liners. Nonetheless, when *Titanic* sailed on her maiden voyage, some 115 members of her crew had close connections to the city. This is according to Liverpool historian Alan Scarth.[2] Meanwhile, control of the company passed to the International Mercantile Marine Company (IMMC),[3] of which it formed the major part.

The IMMC was a US company which owned the share capital of the Oceanic Steam Navigation Company (OSNC), a UK company registered in Liverpool. J. Bruce Ismay of the firm Ismay, Imrie & Co. was Managing Director of the OSNC, which owned all the White Star's ocean liners.

Olympic's keel was laid down on 16 December 1908, and *Titanic*'s keel was laid down three months later on 31 March 1909. *Titanic* took just over two years to build, and her numbered approximately 3,000 men. As regards cost, 'a fixed price contract of £3 million for the pair was agreed at the time of contract signing'.[4]

When *Titanic* was launched on 31 May 1911, she was the largest ship afloat and the largest man-made movable object in the world! *Olympic* was launched five months later on 20 October 1910. The ships were virtually identical, both being 882 feet 6 inches in length and 92 feet 6 inches in the beam (widest point). *Titanic*, however, at 52,310 tons displacement, was marginally heavier than her sister ship *Olympic* of 52,067 tons.

Displacement: the weight of fluid that would fill the volume displaced by the floating ship.[5]

Following *Titanic*'s launch, a year of fitting out followed.

2

Titanic: A Further Description

Hull

The steel plates of *Titanic*'s hull were, in the main, 6 feet wide and 30 feet long, and each weighed up to 3 tons. They were held in place by approximately 3 million rivets.

Bulkheads

Titanic's hull was divided into compartments by 15 bulkheads, labelled A to P from bow to stern. The compartments in this narrative, numbering from bow to stern, are designated 1–16. There were nine steel decks.

There were 15 transverse watertight bulkheads, designated 'A' to 'H' and 'J' to 'P' (there was no bulkhead 'I') from bow to stern, and extending from the double bottom of the ship. The first two bulkheads A and B extended to the height of D deck; the seven bulkheads C to H and J extended only to the height of E deck (one deck lower); the bulkheads K to P, like the forward two bulkheads, extended to the height of D deck.

Were *Titanic*'s watertight bulkheads 'strong enough to resist the pressure of water which would be upon them in the event of one side of them being flooded'? Yes, 'they were so designed', Harland & Wolff's naval architect Edward Wilding replied.[1] However, although the bulkheads were watertight in respect of the flow of water in a lateral direction (that is, provided that the watertight doors contained in each bulkhead were closed), the ceiling of the compartments to which they were attached, were not water were not generally watertight. Once one or more compartments filled with water, this would cause the ship to tilt, and when the ship had tilted sufficiently for the water level to exceed the height of the ceiling (deck) above the compartment in question, water would simply continue to flow upwards through hatches, stairways, conduits etcetera, into the adjacent compartments, setting up a chain reaction.

The idea was that if, say, one of the forward compartments was punctured, allowing the ingress of seawater, then as this sea water began to fill up the lower part of the compartment, the upthrust would be less, and the bows would sink lower in the water. However, the tilt of the ship would be fairly minimal, and the water within the compartment would not rise above sea level. Therefore, it would be nowhere near the height of bulkheads on either side, which would safely contain the seawater, and therefore the safety of the ship would not be compromised. This was estimated to be the case even if two compartments were punctured.

Watertight doors
Each bulkhead was fitted with a watertight door to allow the passage of people and materials between the various compartments.

Said Harland & Wolff's archivist Thomas G. McCluskie, on *Titanic*, and on other White Star vessels, the bulkhead doors 'were of Harland & Wolff's own special design and were hydraulically operated. Each one was of massive construction and fitted with oil cataracts to govern the closing speed'.

Oil cataract: a vertical cylinder with brass plunger. The cylinder is filled with oil, which can only escape through a small adjustable opening. In the 'open' position, the plunger will descend only slowly.

'Each door was held in the open position by a suitable friction clutch. This clutch could be instantly released by means of an electrically operated magnetic switch controlled from the captain's bridge. In the event of an emergency, or at any other time necessary, the doors could be closed throughout the vessel instantly, creating a series of individual watertight compartments.'[2]

In the event of the watertight doors being closed, a warning was given and there was a small, time delay to allow those trapped inside to escape. Otherwise, escape routes were provided by ladders and hatchways within each compartment.

Each bulkhead door could also be closed from below, said Blake, by operating a lever fitted in connection with the friction clutch. As a further precaution, floats are provided beneath the floor level which, in the event of water accidentally entering any of the compartments, automatically lifted and thereby closed the doors opening into that compartment if they had not already been dropped by those in charge of the vessel.[3]

Keel and Double Bottom
Below *Titanic*'s decks was her double bottom. The vessel's outer bottom was flat, the steel plates being laid horizontally, with a slight upward curve

laterally where they joined the sides of the ship. Above the bottom was the inner bottom, or tank top. The double bottom extended from bulkhead A, near the bow, almost to bulkhead P, the last bulkhead towards the stern. Stearn at the stern. The height of the double bottom at the centre keelson (a structure running the length of the ship and fastening the plates of the floor to its keel) was 63 inches, except for the section below the reciprocating engine room, where it increased to 78 inches.

Clearly, the presence of a double bottom meant that if it was perforated, water could not rise above the inner bottom, and therefore could not penetrate further into the ship. However, the situation was more complicated than that.

The centre keel and keelson, which extended from bulkhead B to bulkhead O, and two longitudinal bulkheads each located approximately 30 feet from the centre line and extending from bulkhead D to bulkhead M, subdivided the double bottom longitudinally. Whereas transverse bulkheads, which 'practically coincided with the 15 major transverse bulkheads above, and labelled A-H and J-P, subdivided the double bottom transversely. Thus, 44 watertight compartments – or 'tanks' – were created within the cellular double bottom, plus the fore and aft peak tanks, making 46 in all.

These subdivisions resulted in the following layout. From bulkhead A to bulkhead D, and from bulkhead M to bulkhead P there was a single inner tank on either side of the keelson. However, from bulkhead D to bulkhead M there were additional wing tanks, located to the port and starboard of the two longitudinal bulkheads and extending laterally as far as the ship's sides. And where the wing tanks met the hull, they curved upward to a height of seven feet above the keel. In total there were eight pairs of wing tanks and 15 pairs of inner tanks.[4]

The tanks were watertight and served a variety of purposes. A number of them could be filled with seawater and used to adjust longitudinal trim by shifting water ballast fore and aft. Six of the tanks were used exclusively for the storage of fresh water. Most importantly, the presence of the watertight tanks would, in the event of the double bottom being punctured, prevent the spread of seawater throughout the double bottom, and limit the ingress of water into the main part of the ship.

Said McCluskie, 'The centre keel girder, or spine, for *Titanic* was a hollow box section, 5 ft 3 in. deep, mounted on a flat keel plate 1.5 in thick. Resting on this keel plate was the keel bar itself, a solid bar of 3 in thick steel, which provided the basic hull strength member'.[5]

Keel: the lengthwise steel structure along the base of the ship, supporting the framework of the whole.[6]

Keel plate: flat plate keel – a keel made of flat plate or plates.

Keel bar: steel bar placed along centre of keel to give it its strength.

Beneath the keel was a rubbing strip 19.5 inches wide by 3 inches deep, to serve as protection in the event of the ship grounding.

Finally, there was an external bilge keel 'about 300 feet long and 25 inches deep, fitted along the bilge amidships on both sides of the ship.

Bilge: the area on the outer surface of a ship's hull where the bottom curves to meet the vertical sides.[7]

Bilge keel: each of a pair of plates fastened under the sides of the hull to provide lateral resistance to the water, prevent rolling, and support its weight in dry dock.[8]

3
Titanic's Decks

The Boat Deck (top deck)
The boat deck was located amidships (in the middle of the ship), from forward of the foremost funnel to aft of the aftermost funnel. The height from waterline to boat deck was 60 feet. Of *Titanic*'s four funnels, only the first three were functional, the rear one being merely for show and also to provide ventilation to the bowels of the ship.

On the boat deck, from front to rear, were the officers' promenade; the first class promenade; the engineers' promenade; the second class promenade.

Promenade Deck: an open-air upper deck on which passengers and members of the crew may walk for fresh air and exercise. Aboard *Titanic*, such decks were segregated.

On the forward part of the boat deck was the bridge and wheelhouse (fully enclosed section of the bridge within the main bridge structure). The bridge was the nerve and command centre of the ship, from which the officers controlled and monitored it's direction and speed and kept in contact with the crew by means of telephones. For each four-hour watch, the officer in charge was called the officer of the watch. His duties were to record and guide the ship on its course, monitor the weather, and ensure that the ship's navigation lights were switched on at night. In an emergency, the officer of the watch would always consult the captain. On the bridge, Captain Smith and his officers worked out *Titanic*'s position and course at the chart table, and the captain marked this up on the charts in person.

Titanic possessed three ship's wheels, one contained in the wheelhouse, another in the navigating bridge (located in front of the wheelhouse), and the third on the docking bridge (an elevated platform running the width of the ship and located on the poop deck (on B deck at the stern). It included not only a ship's wheel but also docking telegraphs, a telephone and other equipment to assist in the docking of the ship).

Also within the wheelhouse was the Engine Order Telegraph, which connected directly with the engine room. Its handle was rotated by the officer on the bridge to indicate the desired speed of the ship: 'Stop'; 'Stand By'; 'Dead Slow'; 'Slow'; 'Half'; 'Full'. Whereupon the engineer moved his handle accordingly, to confirm that the order had been received.

Located to the rear of the bridge in succession were the captain's quarters, the officers' quarters, and officers' smoking room. Next came the Marconi Wireless Room (from which messages in Morse code could be transmitted and received); accommodation for some of the first class passengers; the grand staircase for use of the first class passengers; the gymnasium; the officers' mess; the engineers' smoke room; the aft grand staircase, with it glass-domed top to admit light and protect from the weather, and three elevators. Finally came the forward staircase for Second Class passengers.

Promenade ('A') Deck
This was an open deck (i.e. not roofed or enclosed, but open to the air) which afforded excellent views all round. First class accommodation was provided in the vicinity of the first funnel. To the rear of the second funnel were the first class reading and writing rooms, first class lounge, and first class smoke room (for men only, who wished to smoke). To the rear of this were located the Verandah Café and Palm Court, which provided refreshments for the first class passengers.

Deckchairs and steamer rugs (travelling rugs for keeping warm on deck) could be hired for a charge of four shillings per voyage.[1]

Bridge ('B') Deck (inappropriately named, as the bridge was not located here)
Forward was the forecastle deck. Here was the forward mast, used to support the radio antennae and also to carry signalling flags. Attached to the foremast was the crow's nest lookout position, which was located 90 feet above the waterline and 40 feet above the upper deck. Finally, there were two chains to which the ship's anchors were attached. The crow's nest was to play a highly significant part in the events which were to come.

Titanic's three anchors and chains were manufactured at the Hingley Iron Works at Netherton in the Worcestershire, the two side anchors weighing in at 7.8 tons each and the massive central anchor at 15.8 tons.

Most of the midships was taken up by first class accommodation, some of the rooms having en suite bathrooms. Parlour suites, each including a sitting room, were located either side of the second funnel. Next came the first class boarding entrance; galley and pantry; À la Carte Restaurant and Café Parisien providing luxurious meals for first class passengers; the second class smoke room. Finally, at the stern, was the poop deck (raised deck aft). On the bridge deck was the first class promenade (located between the first and third funnels), and the second Class promenade (located fore and aft of the fourth funnel).

Shelter ('C') Deck
This was the uppermost deck to run continuously for the whole length of the ship. Forward were the firemen's, seamen's, and greasers' mess.

Greaser: whose task was to keep the machinery well oiled. Greasers reported to the Second Engineer in charge of each watch.

Next came the well deck (open deck), with two cranes. The area in the vicinity of the first and fourth funnels was given over to first class accommodation, a barber's shop, and the maids' and valets' saloon where the servants took their meals. To the rear of the second class stairway was the second class library. Next came the aft well deck with 2 cranes. To the rear of this were the third class smoke room, general room, and stairway. Finally, at the stern was located the steering gear, including two steering engines, controlled by operating the ships' wheels and used to work the rudder.

Saloon ('D') Deck
Forward was the firemen's accommodation and firemen's staircase, which led right down to Tank Top (lowest deck) where the boilers were located. There were 24 double-ended and five single-ended boilers.[2] Next came the third class promenade; First class accommodation, reception room, and dining saloon. Then the galley and pantry and hospital; second class dining saloon and accommodation; and finally, at the stern, third class accommodation.

Upper ('E') Deck

Forward on the port side was accommodation for engineers, cooks, stewards, waiters, seamen, and trimmers.

Stewards were designated as first class, second class or third class, according to which class of passengers they looked after. However, first class passengers received far more one-to-one attention than those in the second or third class. Stewards cleaned the cabins, prepared the food, and served the meals. A bedroom steward looked after the passengers and their cabins; a pantry steward assisted with the preparation of food; a saloon steward served food to the passengers.

Able Seaman: skilled seamen, whose work nevertheless was often tedious, for example, scrubbing the decks.

Trimmers moved coal from the bunkers to the boilers. Firemen kept the boilers fed with coal. Greasers made sure that the engines were kept well oiled.

Also on the port side was the main thoroughfare used by the crew, otherwise known as 'Scotland Road' (after a street of that name in Liverpool). Also forward was more third class accommodation and the third class entrance. On the starboard side was more first class accommodation, and amidships more second class accommodation. Finally, at the stern, was more third class accommodation.

Middle ('F') Deck

Forward was accommodation for crew members; then more third class accommodation. Next there was a swimming pool and a Turkish bath for the use of first class passengers. Amidships was the third class dining saloon and third class pantry and galley. Further aft was more crew and second class accommodation and finally, at the stern, more third class accommodation.

Lower ('G') Deck

This was the last deck located above the waterline. Forward was accommodation for crew members; then more third class accommodation; first class baggage; post office; and squash racquet court. Amidships were the boiler vents, located below the three working funnels. Aft was the food storage area, and at the stern, more third class accommodation. Even in the third class, cabins had electric lighting, heating, and a wash basin, and at mealtimes passengers received table service.

Orlop Deck
From forward to aft, this deck included cargo and baggage storage; the mail room; the ship's engines; and finally refrigerated cargo.

Tank Top
This was the lowest deck of the ship, which formed the inner bottom of the double-bottomed hull. The tank top provided a platform on which *Titanic*'s boilers, engines, turbines, and electrical generations were housed. It included cargo storage; the firemen's stairs and passage to the six boiler rooms (there being 29 boilers in total). Between each of the boiler rooms were coal bunkers, and the firemen's task was to keep the boilers supplied with coal. Next came two reciprocating steam engines (in which pistons moved up and down in cylinders), each with four cylinders and each three storeys tall. They drove the pistons which rotated the two outermost propellers. The third (central) propeller was powered by a separate engine.

Further aft there were six fresh water tanks; also the Electric Machinery Centre. Steam from the ship's engines was used to supply four 400 kilowatt steam-driven electricity generators, which supplied the entire ship. There were also two 30 kilowatt auxiliary generators, for emergency use.

4
Lifeboats and Safety Equipment

Lifeboats
Of *Titanic*'s 20 lifeboats, which were located on the boat deck, 14 were clinker built wooden boats measuring 30 feet in length and each was designed to carry 65 people. There were two wooden cutters intended for use in an emergency, each of which could carry 40 people. Finally, there were four collapsible Engelhardt lifeboats, rafts made of kapok and cork with heavy canvas sides that could be raised to form a boat. Each could carry 47 people.

Titanic's 20 lifeboats could therefore accommodate a total of 1,178 persons. However, there were almost twice that number of people, 2,209 aboard, on its final voyage. So, the ship's lifeboats could only accommodate about 53 per cent of its human cargo. (Had *Titanic* sailed with her full complement of passengers, which was 3,320, then her lifeboats would only have provided for 35 per cent of her total capacity.) The location of lifeboats was as follows:

Of the 14 clinker-built lifeboats, there were eight aft (four to starboard and four to port), and six forward (three to starboard and three to port). The two cutters were located forward, one on either side of the wheelhouse. Of the Engelhardt lifeboats, one was stored beneath each cutter, and the remaining two were located atop the officers' quarters.

A small crane, known as a davit, was used for suspending or lowering a lifeboat. The davits were 'of the Welin double-acting type manufactured by the Welin Davit and Engineering Co. Ltd, of London. Sixteen sets, specially designed for handling two or, if desired, three boats each, have been provided. Four 15-cwt [hundredweight] electric winches' were provided 'for hoisting and lowering the boats'.[1]

Lifebelts
Titanic's passengers and crew were well provided with lifebelts, there being some 3,500 in all. They were made of canvas and cork. The vessel also carried 48 life rings (ring-shaped life buoys).

Wireless telegraph: 'Marconigrams' and the ability to summon help

The Marconi Room was the nerve centre of the ship in respect of communications with the outside world. Messages in morse code were sent and received by wireless telegraph, which was owned and operated by the Marconi company, and known as 'Marconigrams'. The equipment had a range of 250 miles or more during the day, whereas at night, because of refraction of long-wave radiation in the ionosphere, signals could be sent and received over distances of up to 2,000 miles. During *Titanic*'s final voyage more than 250 telegrams were sent and received, usually weather reports and ice warnings from other ships. These were forwarded to the bridge for the attention of Captain Smith. Outgoing messages were mostly sent by wealthy passengers to their families ashore in England, or in order to book hotels or arrange meetings in New York City. The cost of a telegram was 12 shillings and sixpence for the first 10 words. (*Titanic*'s stewardesses earned 17 shillings *per week*!)

Such a system of communication, which was state of the art on board ship for its time could be invaluable in case of emergency. But how could such an emergency arise, in an unsinkable ship like *Titanic*? Little did *Titanic*'s passengers or crew know that the telegraph would shortly be instrumental in saving hundreds of their lives!

Titanic possessed two Morse signalling lamps, one located on either side of the bridge. In an emergency, they were to be used to flash a signal in Morse code to a would-be rescuer. On a clear night, the Morse lamps had a range in excess of 20 miles.

Rockets

Titanic carried 36 rockets, to be fired sequentially if the ship was in distress. Having been fired, the rocket would rise to a height of several hundred feet before exploding with a loud bang (which alone would have attracted attention) and a brilliant pyrotechnic display like a shooting star.

Whistles

Of *Titanic*'s whistles, of which there were four, only those on the first and second funnels were operational, those on the after two funnels being merely for show. Designed by James Willett Bruce and manufactured by Chadburns Telegraph Company of Liverpool, each weighed a colossal 750 lbs, stood over 4 foot in height, and contained three individual chambers ('pipes') of diameter 9, 12, and 15-inch respectively. They combined to create a powerful sound. The whistles were 'electrically operated, the officer on the bridge having merely to close a switch to give the blast'. The whistles were sounded once a day at noon, in accordance with White Star Line company policy, and also when the ship left port.

There was 'also an electric time-control arrangement, fitted on the Willett Bruce system', whereby the whistles were 'automatically blown for 8 to 10 seconds every minute during thick weather [i.e. when visibility was poor]'.[2] This was to warn other shipping of the vessel's presence.

Could a ship's whistle be used to determine its proximity to ice., Captain Lord of the SS *Californian* was asked (presumably by measuring the echo created when sound bounced off an iceberg)? 'I have read of it, but I have never heard of anyone doing it', he replied.[3]

5

First Class Luxury!

The luxurious facilities provided for *Titanic*'s first class passengers has already been alluded to. However, there was more to come!

Said UK maritime historian John Blake, 'It is impossible adequately to describe the decorations in the passenger accommodation; the ship must be seen and inspected for these features to be fully appreciated. They are on a scale of unprecedented magnificence, nothing like them has ever appeared before on the ocean'.[1]

In this regard, by far the most impressive feature of the ship was the grand staircase. Said McCluskie, 'the main means of moving from deck to deck was by the companionways. There were two for first class passengers, the main companionway – the grand staircase' which was 'located at the forward end of the accommodation alongside the lift', and further aft, another first class companionway, 'extending from the promenade deck to the shelter deck'.

The grand staircase extended down seven levels from the boat deck to decks 'A', 'B', 'C', 'D', and 'E'. At each level was a large entrance hall. It then continued downwards to 'F' deck as an ordinary stairway.

'The main companionway was noted for its grandeur. It was topped by a dome of iron and stained glass, which allowed a flood of light down into the stairwell and onto the landing. The balustrades of the gracefully curving staircase were of iron with occasional touches of bronze in the form of flowers and associated foliage. On the first landing, the plain panelling was embellished with a great carved panel, that contained a clock flanked by the figures of honour and glory crowning time.'[2]

Honour: a male figure, winged and attired in Greek costume, a personification of honour, which was central to the ancient Greek way of life.

Glory: the equivalent female figure, similarly winged and attired.

Time: the Greek God of time was Cronos.

However, for any first class passenger who was unwilling or unable to use the staircase, he or she could always summon a lift, each one having its own lift steward, who opened and closed the doors for the passengers. *Titanic* was equipped with four electric lifts, three in first class and one in second. As for the crew members, they used simple stairways, located behind the scenes and out of sight, to move from deck to deck.

6

Titanic Sets Sail

On 2 April 1912 *Titanic* 'was taken on a short trial run to test the engines and make sure she was seaworthy'.[1] The following day she set sail from Belfast Lough, the large, intertidal sea inlet at the mouth of the River Lagan that connects Belfast to the Irish Sea. She arrived at Southampton at 1.15 a.m. GMT on Thursday 4 April 1912.[2]

The White Star line invited the British Seafarers' Union (founded the year previously in 1911) to select and supply seamen, firemen, trimmers, and greasers for *Titanic*'s maiden voyage. (Other sailors belonged to the National Sailors' Union or to the Firemen's Union.) The Union's aim was to achieve higher wages, shorter hours, better food, and decent sleeping and general accommodation for its members. It provided the following: Shipwreck Benefit; Death Benefit; Accident Benefit, Dispute Pay; Strike Pay; Legal Aid Benefit.

At that time, some 17,000 people were unemployed in Southampton, many of whom applied for work on the *Titanic*, even if they had never been to sea before. Although a few of Southampton's streets were lined with large expensive houses, most people lived in crowded terraces where they struggled to make ends meet. Some 400 of *Titanic*'s crew lived in Chapel and Northam, two of the city's poorest districts. Southampton's factories and docks offered work but not on a steady or secure basis, and many dock workers were hired for one day only.

In the event, 900 or so crew members were signed on and allocated to three departments: the Deck Department, under the direct command of the captain and his officers. This was involved with the sailing and navigation of the ship and keeping her in good repair. The Victualling Department, led by the Chief Steward, whose team looked after the passengers; the Engine Department, which kept the steam turbines going day and night, under orders from the Chief Engineer.[3] Crew members of the Deck and Engine Departments worked four-hour shifts.

Steam turbine: a turbine in which a high-velocity jet of steam rotates a bladed disc or drum.[4]

Meanwhile, in that month of April 1912, coal miners in the UK went on strike for better pay; and without coal, of course, none of the steam-powered ships could sail. Nonetheless, *Titanic*'s 'coaling' took place over a two-day period. A public house called 'The Grapes' on Southampton's Oxford Street was a favourite rendezvous for last drinks before the ship departed.

On Wednesday 10 April at 7.30 a.m. Captain Smith boarded *Titanic*. From 9:00 to 9:30 a.m., lifeboat drill took place.

Titanic sailed from Southampton's White Star Dock soon after 12 noon on Wednesday 10 April, with Trinity House pilot George Bowyer present on the bridge. The estimated time for the journey to New York was six days. The vessel flew the blue ensign (not the red ensign) from her ensign staff at the stern. This reflected the fact that Captain Smith and several of his officers and crew were members of the Royal Naval Reserve (a volunteer force of the UK's Royal Navy).

Trinity House: an association founded in 1514, which was responsible for the licencing of ships' pilots and the construction and maintenance of buoys and lighthouses around the coast of England and Wales.

As *Titanic* was leaving Southampton Docks, she almost collided with the American liner SS *City of New York* (displacement 12,270 tons). More will be said about this shortly.

At about 3:05 p.m. *Titanic* reached the Nab Lightship. Located to the east of the Isle of Wight, this marked the eastern deep-water entry into the Solent (stretch of water separating the Isle of Wight from the mainland). Whether or not the pilot was dropped off here is not certain. In order to save time, he may have remained on board and instead departed the ship at Cherbourg.

Just before 6:30 p.m. *Titanic* dropped anchor within the breakwater of Cherbourg Harbour, in northern France. Here, cargo, mail, and more passengers were collected. At 8:10 p.m. *Titanic* departed for Queenstown in southern Ireland, where more passengers were collected. Overnight the ship's clocks were put back 25 minutes from GMT to synchronise with Dublin Mean Time. On Thursday 11 April at about 1:30 p.m. *Titanic* Time (TT), she departed from Queenstown Harbour.

For reasons that will be explained shortly, the total number of people on board *Titanic* is not known for certain. However, according to the British Board of Trade report, the numbers were as follows:

Passengers:
Men	805
Women	402
Children	109
Total	1,316

Crew:
Men	885
Women	23
Total	908

Total ship's complement 2,224 persons.

At 1:55 p.m. on 11 April *Titanic* reached Daunt Rock off County Cork. This was the official starting point for the trans-Atlantic crossing. That night the ship's clocks were put back by 59 minutes.

At 5:46 p.m. on Friday 12 April *Titanic* received her first warning from the French ship SS *La Touraine* that there was an ice field ahead of her. This was to be the first of several 'ice warnings'. The question was, would Captain Smith heed them?

7

Titanic's Captain, Edward Smith

Edward John Smith was born on 27 January 1850 at 51 Well Street, a modest end-of-terrace house in Hanley, Staffordshire. This was predominantly a coal mining and pottery town, and his father and namesake Edward was a potter, married to Catherine (née Hancock). Smith attended the Wesleyan Chapel and Schools in nearby Etruria, a suburb of Stoke on Trent, and he was a regular attender at Sunday School. Having left school at aged 13, Smith started work at the Etruria forge, as a steam hammer operator.

On 5 February 1867 the 17-year-old Smith travelled to Liverpool and signed on as an ordinary seaman with the 3-masted sailing ship *Senator Weber*, of which his half-brother Joseph Hancock was captain. Centred on the City of Liverpool, Merseyside would now be his home. In 1880, at the age of 30, Smith joined the White Star Line as fourth officer on the SS *Celtic*.

On 13 January 1887, Smith married (Sarah) Eleanor (née Pennington), who bore him a daughter, Helen Melville Smith. In that year, he received his first White Star command, as captain of the SS *Republic*.

During the Second Boer War (1899–1902), Smith served in the Royal Naval Reserve, transporting British Imperial troops to the Cape Colony.

From 1904, Smith became first choice of captain to command the White Star Line's newest ships on their maiden voyages, including RMS *Baltic* (maiden voyage 29 June 1904), *Adriatic* (maiden voyage 8 May 1907), and *Olympic* (maiden voyage 14 June 1911). Meanwhile in 1905, he retired from the RNR with the rank of Honorary Commander.

When the White Star Line transferred its transatlantic headquarters from Liverpool to Southampton in 1907, Smith and his family relocated to that city.

The White Star Line's 'Record of Service in Company' stated that Smith commenced his four-year apprenticeship under the heading 'sail' (rather than steam), his 'Apprenticeship Employer' being 'A. Gibson'. This was a reference to Andrew Gibson, Liverpool shipowner and philanthropist. Also, that Smith joined the company on 1 March 1880. In fact, the number of ships on which Smith served is truly formidable. They are listed as follows:

5th Feb 1867–8th Feb 1868: ship's 'boy' (employed to wait on a ship's passengers or officers) aboard SS *Senator Weber* (1,297 tons).

9th Feb 1868–3rd Sept 1870: 3rd mate (officer) aboard SS *Senator Weber*.

18th Oct 1870–6th March 1871: able seaman aboard the SS *Amoy*.

24th March–15th July 1871: able seaman aboard SS *Madge Wildfire*.

24th Aug 1871–19th Jan 1872: 2nd mate aboard SS *Record*.

28th Feb–27th July 1872: 2nd mate aboard SS *Agra*.

27th Sept 1872–3rd March 1873: 2nd mate aboard SS *Quebec*.

15th July 1873–4th May 1875: mate (first officer) aboard SS *Arzilla*.

May 1876–Jan 1880: Smith's first command, the 3-masted, 1,040 ton SS *Lizzie Fennell*.

March 1880–March 1882: 4th and later third officer aboard the White Star Line's SS *Celtic*. Smith was henceforth employed by the White Star Line.

March 1882–March 1884: second officer aboard SS *Coptic* (Pacific service).

March 1884–July 1885: second officer aboard SS *Britannic*.

July 1885–April 1887: first officer aboard SS *Republic*.

April–August 1887: temporary command of SS *Republic*.

August 1887–February 1888: first officer aboard SS *Britannic*.

April–May 1888: commanded SS *Baltic*. This was Smith's first White Star command.

June–September 1888: commanded SS *Britannic*.

December 1888: commanded SS *Cufic*, a cattle transporter, on her maiden voyage.

January 1889: commanded SS *Republic*.

April–July 1889: commanded SS *Celtic*.

December 1889–February 1890: commanded SS *Coptic* (Australian service).

December 1890–February 1891: commanded SS *Adriatic* (North Atlantic service).

March–April 1891: commanded SS *Runic*.

May 1891–May 1893: commanded SS *Britannic*.

June 1893: briefly commanded SS *Adriatic*.

July 1893–January 1895: commanded SS *Britannic*.

January 1895: briefly back in command of SS *Cufic*.

January–April 1895: commanded SS *Britannic*.

May–June 1895: commanded SS *Germanic*.

July 1895–November 1902: commanded RMS *Majestic* (powered entirely by steam), that made two voyages to South Africa, transporting troops to the Boer War.

December 1902–May 1903: commanded SS *Germanic*, while *Majestic* was refitting.

May 1903–June 1904: commanded SS *Majestic*.

29th June 1904–March 1907: commanded the new RMS *Baltic*.

8th May 1907–February 1911: commanded the new RMS *Adriatic*.

May 1911–March 1912: commanded the new RMS *Olympic*.

April 1912: commanded RMS *Titanic*.[1]

During a career spanning 45 years, Smith had risen from the position of a lowly cabin boy on a sailing ship to become captain of largest ship in the world, with the responsibility for conveying hundreds of passengers across the great Atlantic Ocean. His rise had been truly stellar. The question now was, would he be able to justify the faith placed in him by the Board of the White Star Company, and its Chairman J. Bruce Ismay in particular?

Captain Smith looked the part, not overly tall but burly and of erect posture, with fine white beard, moustache, and sideburns. He had an air of authority and is often seen in photographs as adopting a confident pose with arms folded. When *Titanic* was at sea, he was always either on the bridge, or on call should an emergency arise, and the officers of the watch reported to him throughout the day. It was he who set the ship's course and speed. He was also expected to demonstrate his social skills with *Titanic*'s valued first class passengers, which he did par excellence!

A photograph exists of Captain Smith on board *Olympic* with a Russian wolfhound (Borzoi) 'Ben'. Ben, however, did not sail with his master aboard the *Titanic*. This had been a gift to Captain Smith's daughter Helen from Benjamin Guggenheim, and the captain was clearly delighted to be photographed posing with it. Here was the most famous mercantile marine captain in the world, with a magnificent creature gifted to his family by one of the most famous industrialists in the world! Another photograph exists of Captain Smith, with Lord Pirrie, Chairman of the White Star Line and director of Harland & Wolff, builders of *Olympic* and *Titanic*.

8

Captain Smith: Bravado: Previous Mishaps

In an interview given on 16 May 1907 to reporters in New York, Captain Smith stated as follows: 'When anyone asks me how I can best describe my experience in nearly forty years at sea, I merely say, uneventful. Of course, there have been winter gales and storms and fog and the like. But in all my experience, I have never been in any accident of any sort worth speaking about'.[1] This, of course, was simply untrue.

On 1st May 1898, the *New York Times* reported that RMS *Majestic*, commanded by Captain Smith, had collided with the quay on arrival in New York, sustained broken plates, and sprung a leak.

On 27 January 1899 the *Republic*, under the command of Captain Smith, ran aground off Sandy Hook, on the approach to New York Harbor. 'She was pretty firmly stuck, and it took five hours of vigorous work on the part of the master and crew before the ship was finally refloated.'[2]

On 31 December 1902, Smith, as captain of the *Germanic*, left Liverpool en route for New York. On 10 January 1903, as the ship was travelling along North River en route to her berth in New York Harbor, she 'struck and sank a garbage scow [flat-bottomed boat used for transporting cargo to and from ships in harbour], one of a number being pulled by a tug. The two men aboard the scow, James Mullen and Daniel McCarthey, jumped overboard and grabbing hold of the tow line they managed to pull themselves over onto another scow'.[3]

At 3.20 a.m. on 4 November 1908 the *Adriatic*, captained by Smith, ran aground on a sand bank at the entrance to the Ambrose Channel, on arrival at New York Harbor. 'At 8.10 a.m. the tug *Merrick-Chapman* pulled *Adriatic* free of the sand and towed her into deeper water.' There was no damage to the ship.[4]

On 15 December 1896, said Gary J. Cooper, author of *Titanic Captain: The Life of Edward John Smith*, New York was engulfed in 'a major storm'. A 'severe snowstorm' ensued, with winds of 40 miles per an hour and thick snow offshore. 'By the next morning the weather was still appalling. Two snow-caked steamers had reached Ellis Island [in New York Harbor] that morning, but nothing was leaving the port. The [passenger liners] *St Louis*, *Noorland*, and *Majestic* were docked, and it was doubted that any of them would leave that day. Captain Smith, though, was not daunted by the storm and readied his ship for sea. The *Majestic* left port late on the 16th and sailed straight into the maelstrom'. Whereupon the ship encountered 'ferocious winds, snow, and sleet blasting across the decks', with 'towering waves crashing over the rails, while the passengers locked their doors and otherwise kept below decks as the *Majestic* ploughed on across the Atlantic'. On the third day, 'an iceberg loomed into sight' – an ominous foretaste of things to come! For this would not be the last iceberg that Captain Smith would encounter, but next time it would be in the dark of night and have alarming and serious consequences! The battered ship finally made landfall at Queenstown at 11 a.m. on 24 December.[5]

As *Titanic* was leaving Southampton Docks on 10 April 1912 for her maiden voyage, she almost collided with the American liner SS *City of New York* (displacement 12,270 tons). *Titanic*'s powerful wash served to wrench *New York* from her moorings and as the ship swung towards the *Titanic*, Captain Smith gave the order to stop engines and the two ships only just avoided a collision. One of the attendant tugs now pushed the SS *City of New York* back towards the quayside and *Titanic* sailed on. It seems that either Captain Smith was unaware of the enormous suction that was created at the stern of *Titanic* by virtue of her forward motion, or he simply chose to press on regardless. *Titanic* was now behind schedule by about an hour.

In *Captain E. J. Smith Memorial: A Souvenir of July 29th 1914*, J. E. Hodder Williams of the publishers Hodder & Stoughton, who had crossed the Atlantic with Captain Smith 'on many ships and in many companies', described the captain thus: 'He had an infinite respect – I think that is the right word – for the sea. Absolutely fearless, he had no illusions as to man's power in the face of the infinite'.[6] This, of course, is a contradiction in terms. For example, fearlessness surely indicates a *lack* of respect! Bearing this in mind, the question arises, who appointed Smith to be Captain of the *Titanic*, given his accident-prone track record? The answer, presumably, is the White Star Line's Board of Directors, of which company J. Bruce

Ismay was Chairman and Managing Director, so it is virtually certain that he approved the appointment.

In his book *Titanic and Other Ships*, *Titanic*'s Second Officer Lightoller was generous in his praise of Captain Smith, 'or 'E.J.' as he was familiarly and affectionately known', who he regarded with high esteem. The captain, he said 'was quite a character in the shipping world. Tall, full whiskered, and broad. At first sight you would think to yourself "Here's a typical Western Ocean Captain. Bluff, hearty, and I'll bet he's got a voice like a foghorn". As a matter of fact, he had a pleasant quiet voice and invariable smile. A voice he rarely raised above a conversational tone – not to say he couldn't; in fact, I have often heard him bark an order that made a man come to himself with a bump'.

'He was a great favourite, and a man any officer would give his ears to sail under. I had been with him many years, off and on, in the mail boats, *Majestic* mainly, and it was an education to see him con [nautical term for control, or in this case navigate] his own ship up through the intricate channels entering New York at full speed. One particularly bad corner known as the South-West Spit, used to make us fairly flush with pride as he swung her round, judging his distances to a nicety; she heeling over to the helm with only a matter of feet to spare between each end of the ship and the banks.'[7]

There is an alternative view however, that Captain Smith, in approaching a port 'at full speed', was overconfident, irresponsible, and reckless.

9

Titanic's Officers

Charles Lightoller boarded the *Titanic* two weeks before her maiden voyage and sailed as first officer for her sea trials. As the sailing day approached, however, Captain Smith made Henry T. Wilde, of the *Olympic*, his chief officer. This caused the original chief officer, William Murdoch to step down to first officer, while Lightoller was demoted to second officer. The original second officer, David Blair, was forced to drop out. The remaining officers retained their positions.

Chief Officer Henry Wilde (aged 39)
Henry Tingle Wilde was born on 21 September 1872 at Walton, near Liverpool. His parents were Henry, an insurance surveyor, and Elizabeth (née Jones).

In October 1889, Wilde commenced a four-year apprenticeship with James Chambers & Co. of Liverpool, serving aboard the square-rigged sailing ship *Greystoke Castle*. From the position of third mate aboard the *Greystoke Castle*, Wilde subsequently became third mate aboard the three-masted sailing ship *Hornsby Castle*; third mate and then second mate aboard the steamship SS *Brunswick*; and finally, second mate aboard the SS *Europa*. In 1897, Wilde joined the White Star Line, and served successively on the *Covic*, *Cufic*, *Tauric*, *Delphic*, *Republic*, *Coptic*, *Majestic*, *Baltic*, and *Adriatic*. Meanwhile, in 1898 he married Mary Catherine (née Jones).

On 19 November 1910, Wilde's wife Mary gave birth to twin sons Archie and Richard, both of whom died shortly after birth. On Christmas Eve 1910, Mary herself died, leaving the grief-stricken Wilde to bring up their surviving four children.

In August 1911, Wilde became chief officer of *Titanic*'s sister ship RMS *Olympic*, serving under Captain Edward J. Smith.[1]

First Officer William Murdoch (aged 39)

William McMaster Murdoch was born on 28 February 1873 at Dalbeattie, Kirkcudbrightshire, in south-west Scotland. His parents were Samuel, from a 'long and notable line of Scottish seafarers', and Jane (née Muirhead).

After school, Murdoch commenced a four-year apprenticeship with William Joyce & Company of Liverpool, serving aboard the *Charles Cosworth* and the *St Cuthbert* (which sank in a hurricane), on the South America run. By the age of 23 he had obtained both his Second Mate's Certificate and his Extra Master's Certificate (the highest professional qualification possible).

From 1897–1899 Murdoch served as first officer aboard the *Lydgate*, a four-masted barque (3-masted sailing ship in which the foremast and mainmast are square-rigged), that 'traded from New York to Shanghai'.

In 1900, Murdoch joined the White Star Line and served aboard the *Medic* (with Charles Lightoller); *Runic*; *Arabic*; *Celtic*; *Germanic*; *Oceanic*; *Cedric*; *Adriatic*, and finally as first officer aboard *Olympic* (1911–1912), which was captained by Edward J. Smith, with Henry Wilde as chief officer. Meanwhile on 2 September 1907, Murdoch married New Zealand school teacher Ada F. Banks.[2]

Second Officer Charles Lightoller (aged 38)

Charles Herbert Lightoller was born in Chorley, Lancashire on 30 March 1874. His parents were Frederick, whose family-owned cotton spinning mills, and Sara (née Widdows).

At the age of 13, Lightoller commenced a four-year sea-going apprenticeship, and served aboard the *Primrose Hill*, a steel-hulled, four-masted barque, and the *Holt Hill*, a 4-masted iron ship.

In early 1890, Lightoller sailed aboard the *Primrose Hill*, a 4-masted barque, and subsequently as third officer aboard the windjammer (merchant sailing ship) *Knight of St Michael*, a cargo carrying steamship. In 1895, aged 21, he commenced a career aboard steamships sailing around the West African coast. In the course of his career at sea, during which time he sailed the Atlantic and Indian Ocean and the Southern Seas, Lightoller was dismasted, ran aground, survived a cyclone and a fire aboard ship, and contracted malaria!

In 1898, Lightoller changed direction, relocated to Canada, and became in turn a gold prospector, cowboy, and finally a hobo (migrant worker).

In 1900, having served as third officer on the *Knight Companion*, Lightoller joined the White Star Line. In 1903, he married Australian Sylvia Hawley-Wilson.

Lightoller served aboard the following White Star ships: *Teutonic, Georgic, Cymric, Germanic*, and *Oceanic*, rising from fourth officer to first officer. From December 1911 to March 1912, he served as first officer aboard *Majestic*, under Captain Edward Smith.[3]

Third Officer Herbert Pitman (aged 34)

Herbert John Pitman was born on 20 November 1877 in the village of Sutton Montis, Somerset. His parents were Henry, a farmer, and Sarah (née Marchant).

In 1895, aged 18, Pitman joined the merchant navy, underwent navigation training, and served a four-year apprenticeship, followed by five years as a deck officer.

From 1904 he served one year as a deck officer with the Blue Anchor Line on voyages between England and Australia. He then moved to the Shire Line where he served for six months as a deck officer on voyages from England to Japan.

In 1906, Pitman joined the White Star Line, and served as second officer aboard the *Delphic*; fourth officer aboard the *Majestic*; and fourth officer aboard the *Oceanic*.

Pitman's duties aboard the *Titanic* included working out the ship's position through celestial observation; calculating the deviation of the ship's compass (difference between True North and Magnetic North); general supervision around the decks; looking after the quartermasters and relieving the officers on the bridge whenever necessary.[4]

Fourth Officer Joseph Boxhall (aged 27)

Joseph Groves Boxhall was born in Hull, Yorkshire, on 23 March 1884. His parents were Joseph, a ship's master with the Wilson Line of Hull, and Miriam (née Groves).

In 1899 he commenced an apprenticeship with the William Thomas Line of Liverpool, and sailed to Russia, the Mediterranean, North and South America, and Australia.

In 1903, Boxhall joined the Wilson Line and in 1907, he joined the White Star Line. As sixth officer aboard the *Oceanic*, he met Charles Lightoller. In 1911, he served aboard the *Arabic* on the North Atlantic run. From June 1912, he served as fourth officer aboard the *Adriatic*, William Murdoch being the first officer.[5]

Fifth Officer Harold Lowe (aged 29)
Harold Godfrey Lowe was born on 21 November 1882 in Eglwys Rhos, Conwy, Wales. His parents were George, from a family of jewellers, goldsmiths, silversmiths, and watchmakers, and Emma (née Quick).

In 1911, after five years of voyaging along the West African coast, Lowe joined the White Star Line, and served as third officer on both the *Belgic* and the *Tropic*.[6]

Sixth Officer James Moody (aged 24)
James Paul Moody was born in Scarborough, Yorkshire, on 21 August 1887. His father John was a solicitor married to Evelyn Louisa (née Lammin).

After school, Moody joined the Royal Naval Training Ship HMS *Conway*, stationed in Liverpool's River Mersey, as a cadet. In 1904 he joined the William Thomas Line and served aboard the 3-masted sailing ship *Boadicea* as apprentice. Having served aboard cargo ships and oil tankers, Moody joined the White Star Line in 1911 and served as sixth officer aboard the *Oceanic*, Charles Lightoller being the second officer.[7]

Perhaps the two most significant facts in respect of *Titanic*'s captain and officers are, what a wealth of experience they had accumulated between them, and also how many of them had known and worked with one another on previous ships. This should have made for a harmonious, efficient, and competent team, and a safe voyage for all concerned, surely?

10

Titanic's Crew

The following is a full list, published by *Wikipedia*, of the number of crew members who sailed on *Titanic*.

The Deck Department
This was under the direct command of the captain and his officers, was responsible for the sailing and navigation of the ship and keeping her in good repair. Under this heading were the following:

Boatswain (numbered 1): This was Australian Alfred W. S. Nichols, who assisted Thomas Andrews in his daily inspections of the ship.[1]

Boatswain's mates (2)
Surgeon and Assistant Surgeon: *Titanic*'s surgeon was authorised to make customary charges to his patients.[2]

Able Seamen (29): Able seamen were experienced and skilled, but their work was often tedious, for example, scrubbing the decks.

Masters-at-Arms (2): held the keys to the firearms cabinet.

Quartermasters (7): as petty officers, the seven quartermasters were responsible for steering and signalling. As helmsmen, they steered the ship; or managed signalling with flags; or stood watch on the bridge to assist the duty officer with general navigation. Quartermaster Robert Hichens's task was to pass orders from the officers to the rest of the crew. During his four-hour shift, Hichens would spend two hours at the wheel steering, and two hours standing by ready to deliver messages around the ship from the officer of the watch.

Window cleaners (2)

Lookouts (6): worked two to a shift, each shift being two hours. Archie Jewell, born in 1888, was one of *Titanic*'s six lookouts. His family home was in Cornwall. Jewell first went to sea at the age of 15. He was now aged 23 and had been with the White Star Line for five years.

On 26 March 1912, Jewell left his ship, the White Star liner *Oceanic*, and boarded *Titanic* in Belfast for the voyage to Southampton as a member of her delivery crew. Now, because future employment was not guaranteed, he, like many seafarers looking for their next job, took lodgings in Southampton. He was successful, and a week later he returned to *Titanic* the ship as a seaman, at a standard wage of £5 a month, with an extra 5 shillings for lookout duties. A lookout spent many hours in the crow's nest keeping watch, but he also performed deck duties.

The Engine Department
This department was responsible for keeping the engines, generators, and other mechanical equipment working efficiently, under orders from the Chief Engineer Joseph Bell.

In *Titanic*'s six boiler rooms (or 'stokeholds'), firemen shovelled coal to keep the fires going. This heated the water to create pressurised steam for the engines which worked the propellers. *Titanic* burned more than 850 tons of coal a day, or an average of 35 tons per hour, i.e. approximately 1 ton every two minutes! Under this heading were the following:

Engineers (25): engineers were responsible for keeping the engines, generators, and other mechanical equipment on the *Titanic* running. They were the highest members of the crew and had the highest level of education and technical expertise.

Boilermakers (2): maintained and repaired the boiler systems.

Firemen (13 leading firemen and 163 firemen): otherwise known as stokers, they kept the boilers fed with coal. They were paid £6 a month.

(Coal) trimmers (73): brought coal from the bunkers to the boilers, thereby ensuring that the firemen had adequate supplies near at hand, and carted away ash. The ash was dumped into an injector, which blew it out from the side of the ship. Trimmers also made sure that the trim (balance) of the ship was not altered unevenly. Their shifts were four hours on and eight hours off, and they slept in dormitories, 24 men to a room. Each boiler room had a team of 10 firemen and four coal trimmers.

Greasers (33): their task was to keep the machinery well oiled. They reported to the second engineer in charge of each watch.

Electricians (8): including the Chief Engineer, his Assistant.

The Victualling Department

This was presided over by the Chief Steward whose team looked after the passengers, the dining rooms, and the sleeping quarters. Under this heading were the following:

Purser (1): supervised the Victualling Department and acted as liaison between passengers and ship's officers.

Purser's Clerks (4).

Stewards (322): were responsible for the communal bathrooms, used by all except a few first class passengers; bedrooms, assigned to each class (first, second, or third); shoe shiners ('Boots'), who cleaned and shone the passengers' boots and shoes; 'glory-hole' stewards, who cleaned and maintained the crew's quarters; linen stewards, who washed and maintained all the linen on board. There was also a captain's steward, a gymnasium steward, and a squash court steward. Six mess hall stewards worked in the crew's kitchen to cook and serve their food.

Matron (1) and stewardesses (20): they usually served only the women passengers. Mabel Kate Bennett (née Pilgrim) was born on 22 September 1878 in Eling, Hampshire, to James Pilgrim, labourer, and Sarah Ann (née Groom). She was the seventh of ten siblings.

On 30 April 1905 Mabel was married in St Luke's Church, Southampton to George William Bennett, a taxicab driver. Whereupon the couple relocated to London, where their only child, Mabel Clara, was born on 6 March 1906. The marriage was a failure and after a year, Mabel's husband ceased paying her maintenance. She subsequently wrote to him to say, 'I have waited for years for the keeping of your promise to make a home for me and our child. All these weary years I have been earning sufficient to keep me and the child, but now this is failing. It is true you sent me a few shillings up to the time the child was 12 months old, but nothing since, and I have been left to struggle on alone. I am now writing to again ask you to keep your promise and make a home for us'. But Mabel received no reply.

Mabel returned to Southampton where she stayed with her sister Emily and Emily's husband Alfred Crawford. She now served aboard the *Olympic*. She finally joined *Titanic* as a stewardess, first class, on 6 April 1912.[3]

Mabel's uniform was a dark dress, starched apron, and cap. Her working hours were from 5:30 a.m. to 11:00 p.m. There were no set mealtimes or break times for stewarding staff. 'They just grabbed a break or a bite to eat whenever and wherever they can'. However, at the end of a voyage they might be rewarded by generous tip from a wealthy passenger.[4]

Mabel's story illustrates the kind of hardship, not to say destitution, that less fortunate people were suffering in those days, and how they were willing to take the most arduous and poorly paid of jobs accordingly. There are those who quite rightly decry Britain's former part in the slave trade, but they might reflect on the fact that conditions akin to slavery were all too prevalent on the home front also.

Galley and kitchen staff (62): including chefs, cooks, bakers, butchers, and scullions (dishwashers, who washed and dried the dishes). *Titanic* had three fully equipped kitchens.

Restaurant cashiers (2): both female.

Storekeepers (13).

Ship's Radio operators (2): were employed by the Marconi Company but were also responsible to the ship's captain. *Titanic*'s telegraphist (wireless operator) was John G. ('Jack') Phillips, who had trained at the Marconi Company's training school in Liverpool and worked on several White Star liners prior to joining *Titanic*. His assistant was Harold S. Bride.

Telephone operator (1): *Titanic*'s telephone switchboard was located just forward of the first class lifts on 'C' deck. It had a capacity of 50 lines and was operated by Laurence A. Perkins. From the wheelhouse on the bridge, it was possible to telephone to the forecastle, crow's nest, engine room, and poop. Similarly, it was possible to communicate between the chief engineer's cabin and the engine room, and between the engine room and Nos. 1,2,3,4,5, and 6 stokeholds. There were also telephone connections between 'a number of first class staterooms and also the rooms of the chief officials and various service rooms'.[5]

Barbers (3): all were self-employed and dependent on tips from their customers.

Restaurant (69)
The À La Carte Restaurant, located on B deck, was run as a private concession managed by Gaspare A. P. 'Luigi' Gatti, an Italian businessman. It was open from 8:00 a.m. to 11:00 p.m. but only to first class passengers. The staff included two female cashiers.

Postal clerks (5)
They supervised and processed all incoming and outgoing mail on board ship.

Guarantee Group (9)
Headed by 39-year-old Thomas Andrews, who was a nephew of Lord Pirrie, and Managing Director and Head of the Draughting Department of Harland & Wolff, the group included a joiner, draughtsman, fitter, plumber, electrician, and electrician's apprentice. They sailed aboard *Titanic* in case technical problems arose on the voyage.

Orchestra (8)
The orchestra was contracted to the White Star Line by the Liverpool music agency C. W. & F. N. Black. It operated as a quintet, led by violinist and official bandleader Wallace Henry Hartley, that played at teatime, at

after-dinner concerts, and for Sunday services; and a trio comprising Roger M. Bricoux (French cellist), George Krins (Belgian violinist), and Theodore Brailey (UK pianist) that played at the À La Carte Restaurant and the Café Parisien.

11

Titanic's Passengers

For first class passengers there were '30 suite rooms on the bridge deck and 39 on the shelter deck. In all there are nearly 350 first class rooms, 100 of these being single berth rooms. There is accommodation for over 750 first class passengers. For second class passengers the rooms are arranged as two or four-berth rooms, the total number of second class passengers being over 550'.[1] Most of the second class two or four berth cabins were situated towards the stern. Their furniture was solid and well designed. However, they were cramped, and their occupants were cold as the heating system for second class was not working.

> 'For the third class passengers there are a large number of enclosed berths, there being 84 two-berth rooms. The total number of third class passengers provided for is over 1,100.'[2]

Notable first class passengers included US businessmen Colonel John J. Astor, Benjamin Guggenheim, and Henry S. Harper; US army officer and aide to President William H. Taft Archibald Butt; US businessman and politician Isidor Straus; US businessman and racehorse owner George D. Widener; US civil engineer Washington A. Roebling; US author and journalist Jacques Futrelle; US theatre owner and producer Henry B. Harris; US painter and sculptor Francis D. Millet; US railroad magnate Charles M. Hayes; philanthropist Lucy N. M. Leslie, Countess of Rothes; Scottish landowner Cosmo E. Duff Gordon.

Dining

A typical third class dinner would consist of rice soup, corned beef and cabbage, boiled potatoes, cabin biscuits, fresh bread, peaches and rice.[3] By contrast, a first class dinner offered oysters, consommé Olga, cream of barley, salmon, mousseline sauce, cucumber, filet mignons Lili, sauté of chicken

Lyonnaise, roast duckling, and pâté de fois gras, followed by Waldorf pudding, peaches en Chartreuse jelly, etcetera.[4]

Leisure pursuits

Deck games were popular, but available only to the first and second class passengers. Shuffleboard, for example, was a game in which a long wooden stick was used to aim India-rubber discs at numbers painted on the deck. Quoits was played with rope rings thrown at numbers in concentric circles, or to land as near as possible to a chalk mark.

Titanic's indoor swimming pool was popular with its wealthier passengers, as was the Turkish bath and adjacent shampooing room. In the spacious gymnasium, presided over by an instructor, passengers were offered all the latest exercising devices including running, rowing, and boxing machines, fixed cycles, and even an electric 'camel' – a riding machine that mimicked a camel's gait!

Titanic's bandmaster Wallace Hartley organised live music for the passengers. Rehearsals took place in the morning, and at mealtimes the band performed in the restaurant and in the first and second class dining rooms. A waltz for ships of the White Star Line was specially composed by John C. H. Beaumont, who served as surgeon with the company for 31 years. It was called the 'White Star Waltz'.

Passengers and crew were not the only living creatures aboard *Titanic*, and the charges for the transportation of pets were as follows. Dogs, $10 each; cats and monkeys, provided on application. However, it was stipulated that 'monkeys must be caged before being brought upon the steamer and will then be placed [ominously!] in charge of the butcher'! Pet birds were charged at $2.50 for each cage.[5]

12

Safety: The Board of Trade Passenger Certificate: Failure to Perform a Lifeboat Drill

Before *Titanic* sailed, a Board of Trade Passenger Certificate was required.

At 8 a.m. on Monday 8 April 1912, Board of Trade Emigration Officer Captain Maurice Clarke boarded *Titanic* where, assisted by First Officer Murdoch and Second Officer Lightoller, he carefully checked to make sure that *Titanic* met all the necessary safety requirements.[1]

The day *Titanic* sailed, Wednesday 10 April 1912, was an extremely busy one. At 7.30 a.m. Captain Smith came aboard. At the same time, Captain Clarke boarded the *Titanic* in order to oversee a muster of the crew and a lifeboat drill. In addition, the crew were obliged to undergo a medical inspection. Also present was White Star's Southampton Marine Superintendent Captain Benjamin Steele.[2]

What was a boat muster, as opposed to a boat drill, Marine Superintendent of the White Star Line George A. Bartlett was asked. He replied, 'A boat muster consists of all the men lining up on the deck, and having their names called, and then as they answer their names they proceed to their boats and stand opposite their boats; the officer or petty officer in charge of the boat reads their names over at the boat and reports to the Captain'. The name of each crewman was 'marked on a list opposite a boat with a certain number'.[3] The question is, in the event of an emergency, would the crewmen remember to which lifeboats they had been assigned? After all, one may imagine their mindset, namely one of complacency – i.e. that this was a ship that was unsinkable!

Under his orders, said Lightoller, six of the lifeboats were lowered down into the water and the remainder were lowered part of the way down. The lifeboats were lowered from the boat deck (top deck), which was 60 feet above sea level.[4]

Said Third Officer Herbert Pitman, Lifeboat No. 11, commanded by Fifth Officer Harold Lowe, and Lifeboat No. 13, commanded by Sixth Officer

Moody, each with a crew of 8, now proceeded to row 'around the harbour', before finally rowing back, 'to the satisfaction of the board of trade officials'. The drill took half an hour, from 9:00 a.m. to 9:30 a.m. However, neither the collapsible lifeboats nor the smaller lifeboats were tested.[5] It was further stated that almost all the seamen took part in this lifeboat drill.

There was, however, a problem, said Bartlett, who, at the subsequent UK Inquiry, spoke of a difficulty that he had encountered for 'some 12 months or so', namely the problem of 'the firemen not turning up' for the boat drill. This was a reference to the aforementioned final drill which had taken place before *Titanic* had been cleared to sail. Was there any way in which he could 'make men turn up to go through drill' if they did not wish to do so? 'I am afraid I cannot', he replied. If the boat drill 'were designed to test the boat as to the possibility of lowering her safely with her full load of passengers – I mean as to the falls [wires which enabled the lifeboats to be lowered or raised] being able to bear the strain – that could be done?' 'I think so, yes', Bartlett replied.[6] In fact, such a test had already been performed, on *Olympic* in Belfast on 9 May 1911. Said Wilding: 'We put into one of the lifeboats of the *Olympic* half-hundredweight weights distributed so as to represent a load equal to about 65 people, and then we raised and lowered the boat six times. It was done with the object of testing the electric boat winches, not with the object of testing the boat. I do not think there was any doubt the boats were strong enough to be lowered containing the full number of passengers …'.[7]

It was 'a day or two before Sunday [14 August]', Saloon Steward George F. Crowe confirmed, that he 'saw two notices, one put up in the crew's department – crew's quarters – and one in the first class service pantry'. The notices contained a 'call for muster and fire drill for Sunday at 11.30'. Why was the muster and fire drill not carried out, Crowe was asked? 'Well, I cannot say, with the exception that they held the church service at 10.30 Sunday morning', he replied. The service was over 'soon after 11 o'clock', but 'no explanation given for the suspension of the [fire drill] order'. Nevertheless, the implication was that the church service had taken precedence over the lifeboat and fire drills.[8] Crowe stated that by contrast, on other ships on which he had sailed, it was customary to hold lifeboat drills once a week.[9]

13

The Atlantic Ocean Beckons: 'Tracks'

Just after noon on Wednesday 10 April 1912 whistles were blown on *Titanic*'s two forward funnels indicating that departure was imminent.

The North Atlantic shipping lanes (or 'Tracks') to be taken by ships from 14 January to 14 August each year had been 'agreed to by the principal steamship companies' to 'take effect from 15 January 1899'. A westbound ship must 'steer from Fastnet, or Bishop Rock, on Great Circle course, but nothing South, to cross the meridian of 47° West in Latitude 42° North, thence by either rhumb line, or Great Circle (or even North of the Great Circle, if easterly current is encountered), to a position South of Nantucket Light Vessel, thence to Fire Island Light Vessel, when bound for New York…'.[1]

Fastnet Rock: off the southwest coast of Ireland.

Bishop's Rock: west of the Isles of Scilly.

Great Circle Course: the shortest distance between two points of the globe.

Rhumb line: an imaginary line on the earth's surface cutting all meridians at the same angle, used as the standard method of plotting a ship's course on a chart.[2]

Nantucket Light Vessel: moored south of Nantucket Island, Massachusetts, and stationed south of the Nantucket Shoals and their dangerously shallow waters. The lightship marked the western part of the transatlantic shipping lane, and it was the first lightship to be encountered by westbound liners approaching New York Harbor.

Was *Titanic* sailing 'on its proper course', Third Officer Pitman was asked? 'Yes, sir'. He replied. The 'majority of the big passenger lines', including the

White Star Line, sailed on designated courses ('tracks'). There were 'two different tracks', according to the time of year. One 'is followed from the 14th of August to the 14th of January [i.e. the northern track, as already mentioned], and the other is followed from the 14th of January to the 14th of August. The latter [i.e. the track taken during the coldest months, when icebergs are most prevalent] is the southern track'.[3]

Fifth Officer Harold Lowe stated that he 'worked' [i.e. calculated] *Titanic*'s course from midday on Sunday 14 April until she reached 'what we call the 'corner'; that is, 42° north, 47° west'. As far as he could recall, the ship's course was 60° 33½' west, and it was '162 miles to the corner'.[4]

On *Titanic*'s approach to 'The Corner', said UK systems engineer and *Titanic* researcher Samuel Halpern, she was on a course 240° 6' true (i.e. in relation to the geographic North Pole). From the corner onwards, her intended course was 265° true, as prescribed.[5] This would have brought her to a position just south of the Nantucket Shoals Lightship.

At 5.50 p.m. on the Sunday, *Titanic* had reached the position designated as 'the corner', after which 'South 84 [°] or 86 [°] west would be the true course we were making', said Pitman. 'I am not quite certain which, was the true course.' 'Do you remember the course prior to that?' 'No; I cannot remember it', Pitman replied. He described *Titanic*'s change of course at the corner as 'not a great deal; not a right-angle turn by any means'.[6]

At 10 p.m., said Hichens, 'I had the course given me from the other quartermaster, north 71 west'.[7]

Was *Titanic* sailing 'on its proper course', Pitman was asked? 'Yes, sir.'

The 'majority of the big passenger lines', including the White Star Line, sailed on designated courses ('tracks'). There were 'two different tracks', according to the time of year, said Pitman. One 'is followed from the 14th of August to the 14th of January [i.e. the northern track], and the other is followed from the 14th of January to the 14th of August. The latter [i.e. the track taken during the coldest months] is the southern track'.[8]

At 5.50 p.m. on the Sunday, *Titanic* had reached the position designated as 'the corner', i.e. 47° west and 42° north. 'South 84 [°] or 86 [°] west would be the true course we were making after 5.50; I am not quite certain which, was the true course.' 'Do you remember the course prior to that?' 'No; I cannot remember it', said Pitman. Pitman described *Titanic*'s change of course at the corner as 'not a great deal; not a right-angle turn by any means'.[9] *Titanic* had maintained this new course until she struck the iceberg, said Pitman.[10]

Which track was *Titanic* following, before she struck, the north track or the south track? 'I think she was on the northern track', Lowe replied, though he was far from certain.[11]

Lowe stated that he 'worked' [i.e. calculated] *Titanic*'s course from midday on Sunday 14 April until she reached 'what we call the 'corner'; that is, 42° north, 47° west'. As far as he could recall, the ship's course was 60° 33½' west, and it was '162 miles to the corner'.[12]

14

The Weather and Sea Conditions up to the Night of 14/15 April 1912

Throughout the entire maiden voyage of the *Titanic*, said Second Officer Lightoller, the ship was in 'smooth water'.[1] Fifth Officer Harold Lowe confirmed that throughout the voyage from Southampton, there was 'Fine, clear weather; gentle to moderate breeze and sea'.[2]

On the night of 14/15 April 1912, said Lightoller, the weather was 'clear and calm'.[3] Lookout George T. M. Symons confirmed that on that same night the sea was 'calm'.[4]

At 10 p.m. on the night of 14 April, said Lightoller, when First Officer Murdoch arrived on scene to take over the watch from him, the two of them had a discussion about the current weather conditions. 'We remarked ... about its being calm, clear. We remarked [on] the distance we could see. We seemed to be able to see a long distance. Everything was very clear. We could see the stars setting down to the horizon.[5]

Fourth Officer Boxhall stated that the night was 'perfectly clear'. Did he 'see anything in the nature of haze?' 'No, none whatever', he replied.[6]

Was there any fog that night, Third Officer Pitman was asked? 'No; no fog', he replied.[7] Taylor agreed. There was 'No fog at all' he said. 'Were the stars out?' 'Yes; it was a starry night', he replied.[8] Symons stated that it was 'a very clear night'.[9]

There were, however, differences of opinion as to whether or not there was 'fog' or 'haze':

Haze: a slight obscuration of the lower atmosphere, typically caused by fine suspended particles.[10]

Fog: a thick cloud of tiny water droplets suspended in the atmosphere at or near the earth's surface which obscures or restricts visibility (to a greater extent than mist; strictly reducing visibility to below 1 kilometre).[11]

The Weather and Sea Conditions up to the Night of 14/15 April 1912

When he first came on duty at 10 p.m. on the evening of 14 April, said Lookout Reginald R. Lee, the haze was 'not so distinct then – not to be noticed'. Soon afterwards, however, the lookouts began to 'really notice it. My mate [fellow Lookout Frederick Fleet] happened to pass the remark to me, "Well; if we can see through that we will be lucky". That was when we began to notice there was a haze on the water'. However, 'There was nothing in sight'.[12] Fleet later denied that he had made such a remark, but it is unlikely that Lee would have made the story up.

Although the sky was clear and the stars were shining, said Fleet, 'A sort of slight haze' developed ahead of *Titanic* 'on the waterline … somewhere near seven bells [11.30 p.m. on the evening of 14 April]'.[13]

Some said there was haze and other that there was no haze. So, who was telling the truth? It is likely that they all were, for two reasons. Firstly:

Lookouts

Titanic's lookouts worked in pairs, working 2-hours shifts ('watches') in the crow's nest at regular times each day.

Watch: a fixed period of duty, during which a crew member is stationed to look out for danger or trouble, typically at night.[14]

For *Titanic*'s lookouts, the shifts were arranged as follows:

Evans and Hogg: a.m. midnight–2; 6–8.
    p.m. noon-2; 6–8.
Symons and Jewell: a.m. 2–4; 8–10.
    p.m. 2–4; 8–10.
Fleet and Lee: a.m. 4–6; 10–noon.
    p.m. 4–6; 10–midnight.

Senior Officers

Titanic's senior officers also worked shifts, but of 4 hours, as follows:

Wilde: a.m. 2–6.
    p.m. 2–6.
Murdoch: a.m. 10–2.
    p.m. 10–2.
Lightoller: a.m. 6–10.
    p.m. 6–10.

Junior Officers and Able Seamen

The junior officers on board *Titanic* were required to keep watch with the able seamen. 'Third Officer Herbert Pitman was in charge of the "port watch" and was paired with Fifth Officer Harold Godfrey Lowe. Fourth Officer Joseph Groves Boxhall was in charge of the 'starboard watch' and was paired with Sixth Officer James Moody.' Each watch worked 4 hours on and 4 hours off, but to ensure that the same watch section 'didn't have to work the same hours every day, the 4-hour period from 4 p.m. to 8 p.m. was divided into two Dog Watches of 2 hours each'.[15]

Clearly therefore, no one lookout or person on watch could be on duty all the time and it is possible that, whereas observable haze was present during one shift, there may have been no observable haze during another.

Secondly, haze is not a constant phenomenon. It can come and go, depending on when and where the cold and warm currents meet, and also on the wind's strength and direction.

UK marine ecologist Dr Samantha Andrews described how 'the foggiest place in the world is just off the coast of Newfoundland, Canada in an area of the Atlantic Ocean called the 'Grand Banks'. Here, the somewhat frigid Labrador Current meets the balmy Gulf Stream. When the two air masses meet, the Labrador Current air cools the Gulf Stream air, causing its water vapour to condense'. The moist air condenses 'onto tiny particles (like dust or ice)' or onto 'tiny salt crystals' thrown up by the sea. This creates mist or fog. Fog has a higher density than mist, 'the internationally agreed boundary where mist ends and fog starts' being '1,000 meters. If you can't see beyond 1,000 meters then it's fog'.[16] So, the 'haze' referred to by the various observers aboard *Titanic* was in fact mist.

The likely conclusion is therefore that there was intermittent, light haze during the evening of 14 April 1912. However, this had no material effect on the cataclysmic events which were shortly to befall RMS *Titanic*.

15

Sunday 14 April 1912: Captain Smith's Instructions to his Officers and Their Instructions to *Titanic*'s Lookouts: What They Saw

Quartermaster Robert Hichens stated that he went on watch at 8 p.m. on the evening of 14 April. Said he, 'I heard the second officer [Lightoller] repeat to Mr Moody, the sixth officer, to speak through the telephone, warning the lookout men in the crow's nest to keep a sharp lookout for small ice until daylight and pass the word along to the other lookout men'.[1]

Third Officer Pitman was on watch from 6 p.m. to 8 p.m. on that same. 'We were keeping a special lookout for ice', he said. Did he see any icebergs or evidence of ice during this period? The answer was no.[2]

Lookout George A. Hogg was on watch from 6 p.m. to 8 p.m. (with his colleague Lookout Alfred F. Evans). He was instructed 'to keep a sharp lookout for ice'. He was subsequently asked, 'Did you discover any ice?', he was asked. 'None, sir', he replied.[3]

From the time he came on watch at 8 p.m., had Fourth Officer Boxhall encountered the captain? From 9 p.m. onwards, he replied, until his watch ended at 10 p.m., he had seen the captain frequently. Captain Smith was 'sometimes in his chart room and sometimes on the bridge, and sometimes he would come to the wheelhouse, inside of the wheelhouse. Taking the whole bridge together; all the chart rooms, and the open bridge', said Boxhall, 'they are all practically on one square, and I do not think the captain was away from that altogether'.[4]

Lightoller confirmed that Captain Smith had arrived on the bridge at 8.55 p.m. The Captain 'made a remark that if it was in a slight degree hazy there would be no doubt we should have to go very slowly'. Finally, the captain's parting words before leaving at 'about 20 minutes past 9, or something like that' were, 'If in the slightest degree doubtful, let me know'.[5] In pitch darkness, however, such warnings were irrelevant!

As McCluskie pointed out, bulkhead doors were 'normally left open under normal conditions, but whilst steaming through icebergs they should have been closed'.[6] And yet Captain Smith gave no such order.

16

Titanic's Lookouts: Their Previous Experience and Capabilities

Titanic's six lookouts operated in pairs in the ship's crow's nest and were paid £5 per week, plus an extra 5 shillings in recognition of their added responsibility.

Alfred Evans (aged 25)
Alfred Frank Evans was born on 3 February 1887 in Southampton to parents Charles, a stevedore, and Elizabeth (née Russell). In 1906 he joined the Royal Naval Reserve. From October 1911 to March 1912, he served as able seaman on the White Star Line's *Oceanic*. In 1912 he married Charlotte ('Lottie') Martin.[1]

George Hogg (aged 29)
George Alfred Hogg was born in Kingston upon Hull, Yorkshire, on 7 March 1883 to parents James, a stationary engine driver and house decorator, and Lucy (née Everington). Having gone to sea aged 16, Hogg had occupied various positions, including able seaman, quartermaster, and boatswain's mate, with various shipping companies including the P&O Line, Royal Mail Line and Union Castle Line. In 1906, he married Ada Jeanes.

For the last 4 years, Hogg had been employed by the White Star Line, but the only occasion on which he had been a lookout was on a single voyage with the *Adriatic*. He first joined the crew of *Titanic* in Belfast.

George Symons (aged 24)
George Thomas MacDonald Symons was born on 23 February 1888 in Weymouth, Dorset to parents Robert, fireman on a steamship, and Bessie (née Newman). He had gone to sea at the age of 15 and for the last four years had served aboard White Star Line's *Oceanic*, for three of these years as a lookout.

Archie Jewell (aged 23)
Jewell was born in Bude, Cornwall on 4 December 1888 to parents John, a sailor, and Elizabeth (née Hooper). He went to sea aged 15 years and served aboard sailing ships. Before joining *Titanic*, by which time he had married Bessie Head, he had served for the previous seven years aboard the White Star Liner *Oceanic*.

Frederick Fleet (aged 24)
Fleet was born on 15 October 1887 in Liverpool. Of all *Titanic*'s lookouts, he had the worst possible start in life.

His mother Alice abandoned him as a baby and emigrated to the USA. He never discovered who his father was. Fleet was brought up by a succession of foster parents, in orphanages, and in Dr Barnardo homes for destitute children. At the age of 12 he joined a training ship, the *Clio* (formerly a Royal Naval corvette) at Anglesey in North Wales. Its superintendent was Commander Frederick C. G. Longdon.

At the age of 16 Fleet went to sea and rose to be able seaman. He joined *Titanic* in Belfast. Prior to this, he had served with the White Star Line for some seven years, the previous four of which he had spent as lookout aboard the *Oceanic*.

Reginald Lee (age 41)
Reginald Robinson Lee was born in Bensington, Oxfordshire on 19 May 1870 to parents William and Jane (née Jackson), who were both schoolteachers. Of all *Titanic*'s lookouts, his start in life was the most promising, and yet he failed to take full advantage of it.

In 1887 Lee joined the Royal Navy as a clerk and in 1891 he was promoted to paymaster. In 1897 he married Emily Hill. However, in 1900 he was discharged on account of problems with alcohol.

Prior to joining *Titanic*, Lee had served aboard the Royal Naval corvette HMS *Cordelia*; the US-owned Atlantic Transport's ocean liner *Minnehaha*; and finally, the White Star liner *Olympic*.

Tests of vision
Hogg stated that his eyes had been tested 'about two months' previous to *Titanic*'s sailing.[2] Symons stated that the previous September, his eyes 'were

Titanic's Lookouts: Their Previous Experience and Capabilities

tested by the Board of Trade by the new test, the latest test out'. He also confirmed that he was given 'a certificate' stating that he was 'qualified as a good lookout'.[3] Fleet stated that his eyes had been tested at Southampton 'a couple of years or a year' ago by the Board of Trade. However, he had mislaid the relevant certificate.[4] It is likely that the remaining lookouts had undergone similar tests.

17

The Mystery of the Missing Binoculars

Lookout George A. Hogg stated that when he signed on as *Titanic* was leaving Belfast, he was issued with a pair of binoculars for use in the crow's nest, by Mr Blair, the second officer. They were marked, for use in 'Theatre [i.e. playhouse], Marine and Field. Second Officer, S.S. *Titanic*'. In other words, they were multi-purpose, for use in the theatre, at sea, or in the great outdoors.

However, on arrival at Southampton, 'Mr Blair was in the crow's nest and gave me his glasses and told me to lock them up in his cabin and to return him the keys'. So, there were subsequently no glasses for use in the crow's nest.[1]

Lookout Frederick Fleet testified that there were binoculars in the crow's nest during the voyage from Belfast to Southampton. But were they 'taken from you at Southampton?' he was asked? To this he replied, 'Yes'. By contrast, during his four years' service as a lookout man aboard the *Oceanic*, he had glasses 'every trip'.

Lookout Reginald Lee had previously acted as lookout man in other ships, notably on mail steamers. In that capacity, he had used 'glasses' – i.e. binoculars. Had he found them to be of use? 'They are better than the ordinary eyesight', he replied. He then explained that the binoculars used at night-time – 'night glasses' – were different from those used during daylight hours. In fact, binoculars issued by the White Star Line were manufactured by the company Sharman D. Neill of Belfast. They had three lenses of three different focal length, which could be selected by revolving a button on the side. There were evidently no 'night glasses' as such.

Lee confirmed that binoculars were supplied to ships of the White Star line. His fellow lookout man ('mate') aboard the *Titanic*, Fleet, who had served for four years as look-out man aboard the *Oceanic*, told him that 'they had them there' and 'used them there'. Now came a crucial question. Were any binoculars supplied to the lookout men aboard the *Titanic*? 'No, not for our use anyway', Lee replied. 'Was there any place in the crow's-nest for glasses?' 'Yes, there was – a small box.' 'If I understand you aright, there was a box there for glasses, but no glasses in the box?' 'I could not tell you if they were for glasses, but there was a box there that would hold glasses.'

Lee was asked if he had searched the crow's nest for binoculars. No, but 'we asked for them'. Who was 'we'? This was one of Lee's colleagues, either Jewell, or Simmons [Symons], who was 'Jewell's mate on the lookout'. And the reply? 'They said there were none for us.'[2]

Lee reported a conversation between himself and fellow lookouts, Fleet, Hogg, Evans, and Symons, which had taken place in the crow's-nest when *Titanic* was en route from Belfast to Southampton. They could not understand why the binoculars that they had used during this part of the voyage had simply 'vanished at Southampton'. Where had they gone? Lee simply did not know. What was the outcome? 'We did not have any to use. We simply went without them.'[3]

Said Hogg, 'I have always had night glasses in the White Star boats', but this was not the case aboard *Titanic* after she had left Southampton. Yet he had 'asked for the glasses several times'. By contrast, he said, the officers on the bridge did have glasses.[4]

'When keeping a lookout for icebergs aboard the *Oceanic*', Symons was asked, did he use 'glasses' – i.e. binoculars? The answer was yes. These were 'an ordinary pair of glasses' and not 'special glasses for night', and they were kept in a box in the crow's nest. And did he find them useful? 'Yes; very useful' Symons replied. 'Were there any binoculars on the *Titanic*? 'No, none whatever. After we left Southampton and got clear of the Nab Lightship, I went up to the officers' mess room and asked for glasses. I asked [Second Officer] Mr Lightoller, and he went into another officers' room, which I presume was [First Officer] Mr Murdoch's, and he came out and said, 'Symons, there are none'. With that I went back and told my mates.'[5]

Had Fleet made 'any request for glasses [binoculars] prior to *Titanic* embarking from Southampton? 'We asked them', he replied, and 'they said there was none intended for us. 'Whom did you ask?' 'We asked Mr Lightoller, the second officer.' 'Did you make the request yourself?' 'No; the station lookout men did, Hogg and Evans.' How did he know this, Fleet was asked? 'Because they told us', he said. And yet on the voyage from Belfast to Southampton the lookouts *did* have glasses. So, where were they? 'We do not know that', Fleet replied. 'We only know we never got a pair.'[6]

After *Titanic* left Queenstown, said Hogg, he asked Lightoller in person, 'Where is our look-out glasses, Sir?', to which the reply came, "Get them later", or something like that'. 'At any rate, you did not get any?' Hogg was asked. 'I did not get any', he replied.[7]

Lookout Symons had crossed the Atlantic to New York 'roughly about 58 to 60' times, he said, both as 'an able seaman' and also as 'look-out man' for three years aboard the *Oceanic*.[8] He stated that it was the custom for lookouts on ships of the White Star Line to be issued with glasses. He himself had 'served three years and five months on the *Oceanic*', and he confirmed that its lookouts 'had glasses all the time'.[9]

Prior to joining *Titanic* as an Able Seaman, Thomas Jones had served as a lookout for 'about 12 months' on the *Majestic*, and subsequently on the *Oceanic*. Had he 'ever known a crow's nest to be without glasses?' 'No, sir', he replied. 'We always used to go to the office and get them when we left the port, take them into the crow's nest, and then upon arriving at port again, take them into the office. I never saw a crow's nest without glasses.' However, when the ship was in port, the glasses were kept in 'the office'. If they were left in the crow's nest, 'somebody might steal them there'.[10]

Why no binoculars were available to the lookouts in *Titanic*'s crow's nest, when they were available on all other White Star liners, remains a mystery, as does the fact that none of the ship's officers thought the matter of sufficient importance to warrant them intervening and putting matters to rights. What impact this glaring omission would have in the tragic events which were shortly to follow, remained to be seen.

18

Warnings of Ice and Icebergs, Some of Which Did Not Reach the Bridge, and All of Which Captain Smith Chose to Ignore

The following ships sent warnings to *Titanic* about the presence of ice in the vicinity of the route ('track') which the ship was following. Furthermore, UK researcher Paul Lee has produced a series of informative diagrams, showing the relevant time at which these warnings were received by *Titanic*, a plot of her course, and her position relative to the ice. The times given are '*Titanic* Time' (TT), rather than Greenwich Mean Time (GMT) or New York Time (NYT) unless otherwise stated.[1]

Calculations are based on the fact that at 45 degrees North (the circle of latitude that is 45 degrees north of Earth's equator), 5 degrees of longitude equates to about 240 miles; and 5 degrees of latitude equates to about 345 miles.

SS *La Touraine* (French)
At 5.46 p.m. on Friday 12 April 1912, *Titanic* received the following message (Marconigram telegram) from SS *La Touraine*. It was prefixed by the acronym 'M.S.G.' (Masters' Service Gram – which required the captain personally to acknowledge receipt of the message):

'To Capt. *Titanic*. My position 7 p.m. G.M.T. [5.36 p.m. TT] lat. [latitude] 49.28 long. [longitude] 26.28 W. dense fog since this night crossed thick ice-field lat. 44.58 long 50.40 'Paris' saw another ice field and two icebergs lat. 45.20 long. 45.09 'Paris' saw a derelict [abandoned ship] lat. 40.56 long. 68.38 'Paris' please give me your position best regards and bon voyage. Caussin.'

Paris: City of, a reference to the Paris Meridian. A small correction was necessary to obtain the position of the ice with respect to the Greenwich Meridian.

Charles-Fernand Caussin, Captain of SS *La Touraine*.

At 6.21 p.m. Captain Smith replied as follows:

> 'To Capt. *La Touraine*, Thanks for your message and information. My position. 7 p.m. G.M.T. Lat. 49.45; long. 23.38. W. Greenwich; had fine weather; compliments. – Smith'

It is significant that Captain Smith's message contained no acknowledgment of Captain Caussin's ice warning.

At 7 p.m. on 12 April, *Titanic* was about 910 miles from the nearer of the two ice fields, as indicated by SS *La Touraine*, or 36 hours steaming time and travelling at a speed of 22 knots. Had the ice and icebergs which Captain Caussin had warned about remained static, *Titanic* would have passed about 170 miles to the east and 100 miles to the south of them. However, ice fields and icebergs *do not* remain static!

SS *Caronia* (UK)
At 9.12 a.m. on Sunday 14 April, *Titanic* received the following message from SS *Caronia*:

> 'Captain, *Titanic*. West-bound steamers report bergs, growlers, and field ice in 42° N., from 49° to 51° W. April 12. Compliments. Barr.'

Growler: A growler was an iceberg which was 'low lying', said Fourth Officer Boxhall – i.e. it did not rise much above the surface of the water.[2]

Field Ice: was defined by Boxhall as 'a large expanse of ice covering the water ... not unlike a raft'.[3]

James Clayton Barr, Captain of the SS *Caronia*.

At 10.28 a.m. Captain Smith replied as follows: 'Captain *Caronia*. Thanks for message and information. Have had variable weather throughout – Smith'.

Again, there was no acknowledgment of *Caronia*'s ice warning, let alone any indication that Captain Smith had taken notice of it.

At the time of SS *Caronia*'s message, *Titanic* was about 295 from the icebergs mentioned in *Caronia*'s message, or 11½ hours away. Had the icebergs which Captain Barr had warned about remained static, *Titanic* would have passed about 96 miles to east and 17 miles to the south of them.

SS *Noordam* (Netherlands)/SS *Caronia* (UK)

At 11.47 a.m. on Sunday 14 April the following message from the SS *Noordam* was relayed to the *Titanic* via the SS *Caronia*:

> 'Captain SS *Titanic*. Congratulations on new command. Had moderate westerly winds, fair weather, no fog. Much ice reported in lat. 42° 24' to 42° 45' and long. 49° 50' to 50° 20'. Compliments. Krol.'

Watze Krol, Captain of the SS *Noordam*.

At 12.31 p.m. Captain Smith replied genially, but remained uncommitted, as follows:

> 'Captain *Noordam*. Many thanks. Had moderate variable weather throughout. Compliments. Smith.'

At the time of SS *Noordam*'s message, *Titanic* was about 250 miles from the ice which Captain Krol had warned about, or about 10 hours steaming time. Had this ice remained static, *Titanic* would have passed about 165 miles to the east and 40 miles to the south of it.

SS *Amerika* (Germany)

At 1.49 p.m. on Sunday 14 April *Titanic* received this message from the SS *Amerika*:

> 'To the steamer *Titanic*. M.S.G. via Cape Race to the Hydrographic Office, Washington DC. *Amerika* passed two large icebergs 41° 27' N., 50° 8' W., on the 14th April. Knuth.'

Cape Race: wireless station located at the south-eastern tip of the Avalon Peninsula, Newfoundland.

H. Knuth, Captain of the SS *Amerika*.

This message evidently did not reach *Titanic*'s bridge.

At the time of the SS *Amerika* message *Titanic* was about 235 miles from the icebergs which the SS *Amerika* had warned about, or about 9 hours steaming time. Had these icebergs remained static, *Titanic* would have passed *only about 17 miles* to the north of them.

RMS *Baltic* (UK)/SS *Athinai* (Greek)
At 1.54 p.m. on 14 April *Titanic* received the following message from RMS *Baltic*, which was relayed to the *Baltic* by the SS *Athinai*:

> 'Captain Smith, *Titanic*. Have had moderate variable winds and clear fine weather since leaving [Liverpool]. Greek steamer *Athenai* reports passing icebergs and large quantities of field ice today in lat. 41° 51' N., long. 49° 52' W.' The message ended, 'Wish you and *Titanic* all success. – Commander.'

The 'Commander' was Joseph Barlow Ranson, Captain of RMS *Baltic*.

At 2.57 p.m. Captain Smith replied as follows:

> 'Commander *Baltic*. Thanks for your message and good wishes; had fine weather since leaving. Smith.'

Once again, Captain Smith failed to thank Captain Ransom for warning him about ice and icebergs in the vicinity, or even to acknowledge that he had done so.

At the time of RMS *Baltic*'s message, *Titanic* was about 220 miles from the ice and icebergs which RMS *Baltic* had warned about, or about 9 hours steaming time. Had the icebergs and ice remained static, *Titanic* would have passed only a mere 6 miles to the south of them.

SS *Californian* (UK)/SS *Antillian* (UK)

At 7.37 p.m. on 14 April *Titanic* intercepted the following message from the SS *Californian* to the *Antillian*:

> 'Captain *Antillian*. 6.30 p.m. ATS lat. 42.3 N, long. 49.9 W. Three large bergs five miles to southward of us. Regards, Lord.'

Stanley Phillip Lord, Captain of the SS *Californian*.

Assistant Telegraphist Harold Bride delivered this message to the bridge, but it was evidently not acknowledged.

At the time of SS *Californian*'s message, *Titanic* was only about 55 miles from the icebergs which SS *Californian* had warned about, or about 2 hours steaming time. Had the icebergs and ice remained static, *Titanic* would have passed *only a mere 11 miles* to the south of it.

SS *Mesaba* (UK)

At 9.52 p.m. on Sunday 14 April, *Titanic* received the following message from Captain Owen Percy Clarke of the SS *Mesaba*:

> 'Ice report in latitude 42° N. to 41° 25' N, longitude 49° W. to longitude 50° 30' W. Saw much heavy pack ice and great number large icebergs. Also field ice. Weather good, clear.'

This message was acknowledged by *Titanic*'s telegraphist Jack Phillips, but it evidently did not reach the bridge and Second Officer Lightoller stated that he did not recall receiving it.

Titanic had now reached the eastern boundary of the ice field which SS *Mesaba* had warned about.

SS *Californian* (UK)

At 10.55 p.m. on 14 April *Titanic* received the following message from the SS *Californian*:

'I say, old man, we are stopped and surrounded by ice.' Whereupon *Titanic*'s telegraphist Jack Phillips replied: 'Shut up, shut up. I am busy. I am working Cape Race'.

What is striking about the above account is the sheer number of ice warnings sent to *Titanic* by ships in the vicinity and how, in his replies, Captain Smith failed to acknowledge them, let alone have the courtesy to thank their senders. Instead, he preferred to talk about the weather!

19

Aboard *Titanic*, was there any Inkling of Ice of Icebergs in the Vicinity?

Fourth Officer Boxhall stated that the temperature of the air and of the seawater were 'taken every two hours after the ship left port' and the results were entered into the ship's log. The log, however, did not survive.[1]

Said Lookout Hogg, 'it was very, very cold, and I said, "There is plenty of ice about here, because it is so cold". That is what I said to my mate'. In other words, to Hogg, an experienced mariner, the presence of bitterly cold weather was an indication of the likelihood that there was ice in the vicinity.[2]

Did Hichens have any reason to suppose that there were icebergs in the vicinity of *Titanic*? Yes, he said, because 'It began to get very, very cold; exceedingly cold; so cold we could hardly suffer the cold. I thought there was ice about, somewhere'.[3]

US first class passenger Ella Bertha Stuart White (née Holmes), widow of John Stuart White, former businessman of Manhattan, was adamant that cold weather meant only one thing. 'Everybody knew we were in the vicinity of icebergs. Even in our staterooms it was so cold that we could not leave the porthole open. It was terribly cold. I made the remark to Miss [Maria Grice] Young, on Sunday morning: 'We must be very near icebergs to have such cold weather as this'. It was unusually cold.'[4] So even the passengers were aware of the danger!

When Captain Lord of the *Californian* was asked if cold air and water indicated the presence of ice, he replied, not necessarily, but it did indicate that the vessel in question was 'in the Arctic current'.[5] In other words, extra caution was needed.

20

Who was On Watch on that Fateful Night of 14/15 April 1912? First Sight of the Iceberg

Titanic's officers

Said Second Officer Lightoller, Captain Smith arrived on the bridge at 8.55 p.m. 'If in the slightest degree doubtful, let me know', were the captain's parting words before leaving at 'about 20 minutes past 9, or something like that'.[1] Prior to this, Captain Smith had been attending a dinner party. How, in these circumstances, 'the millionaire's captain', as he was known, could calmly sit down for an evening meal with his first class passengers, however adoring of him they were, beggars belief!

Third Officer Pitman was on watch from 6 p.m. to 8 p.m. on the evening of Sunday April 14. Did he see any icebergs or evidence of ice during this period? The answer was no. The first ice that he saw was when he was in the lifeboat, at 'about half-past 3 Monday morning'.[2]

Between 7.30 p.m. and 7.40 p.m. that evening, said Pitman, he and Lightoller made observations which included the speed of the ship, which was measured at 'about 21+ knots per hour', according to 'the log and the revolutions [per minute of the propeller shafts]'. 'Were you trying to reach 24 knots', Pitman was asked. No, he replied, 'We had not the coal to do it'. The faster a ship travels, greater is the rate at which coal is used up.[3]

Fourth Officer Boxhall was on watch on *Titanic's* bridge from 4 p.m. to 6 p.m., together with 'Mr Wilde, the chief officer, and Mr Moody, the sixth officer'.

Titanic's quartermasters

Hichens stated that he went on watch at 8 p.m. Said he:

> 'I heard the second officer repeat to Mr Moody, the sixth officer, to speak through the telephone, warning the lookout men in the crow's nest to keep a sharp lookout for small ice until daylight and pass the word along to the other lookout men.'[4]

Titanic's lookouts

Lookout Frederick Fleet stated that he came on watch at 10 p.m. on the Sunday night of 14 April 1912, and that Reginald Lee was his fellow lookout man. Prior to coming on watch at 10 p.m., he said, his previous watch had been from 4 p.m. to 6 p.m. Neither Hogg and Evans, nor Symons and Jewell, who had been on watch in the meantime (from 6 p.m. to 8 p.m. and from 8 p.m. to 10 p.m. respectively) had seen any ice or icebergs.[5]

Iceberg!

When his 2-hour watch was nearly over [i.e. at midnight], said Fleet, 'I reported an iceberg right ahead, a black mass'.[6] 'Was it high above the water or low?' he was asked. 'High above the water', he replied.[7] Fleet immediately 'struck three bells', which, he said, 'denotes an iceberg right ahead'. Then I went straight to the telephone and rang them up on the bridge'. The telephone was answered at once, and he was asked, 'What did you see?'.[8] He replied, 'Iceberg right ahead', he said. 'Thank you' was the reply.[9]

The iceberg 'kept getting [i.e. appearing] larger as we were getting nearer it', said Lee. 'It was a dark mass that came through that haze', he said, 'and there was no white appearing until it was just close alongside the ship, and that was just a fringe at the top. That was the only white about it.'[10]

Fleet's account therefore confirms that yes, there was a degree of haze at that crucial time. And the reason why the iceberg looked white when it was alongside *Titanic* was that it was lit up by the ship's lights. Finally, said Fleet, the iceberg 'was a little bit higher than the forecastle head', i.e. about 50 feet above the waterline.[11]

'All went along very well until 20 minutes to 12', said Quartermaster Hichens, 'when three gongs came from the lookout, and immediately afterwards a report on the telephone, 'Iceberg right ahead'.' Whereupon he heard the telegraph bell ring (indicating that the telegraph order had been acknowledged) and the order 'Hard a starboard', an order which was repeated. 'But, during the time', he said, *Titanic* 'was crushing the ice, or we could hear the grinding noise along the ship's bottom'.[12] In other words, the turn had come too late, and the collision had occurred.

At the sound of the telegraph bell, said Hichens, and Captain Smith 'came rushing out of his room ... and asked, 'What is that?'. Mr Murdoch said, 'An iceberg''. The captain now gave the order, 'Close the emergency [bulkhead] doors'. 'The doors are already closed', said Murdoch. Within '5 to 10 minutes', *Titanic* developed 'a list of 5' to the starboard'.[13]

How far distant from *Titanic* was the iceberg when Lee first caught sight of it? 'It might have been half a mile or more; it might have been less', he replied. 'I could not give you the distance in that peculiar light.'[14]

… Part II

Nemesis

21

The Collision: The Fatal Turn to Port

Fourth Officer Boxhall was asked to state the exact time that *Titanic* had struck. There was some question about it, he replied. 'Some say 11.45 [p.m.], some say 11.43 [p.m.]. I myself did not note it exactly, but that is as near as I can tell I reckoned it was about 11.45.'[1]

Was *Titanic* on the correct 'track'?
Third Officer Pitman was asked if he knew *Titanic*'s latitude and longitude when she struck the iceberg. 'Yes, sir', he replied. And 'did that indicate to you that she was on the true course?' 'Exactly. She was right on the line.' In other words, *Titanic* was following the southern, designated track, as laid down for that time of the year.[2]

'In the position where we sank', said Pitman, the distance between the northerly track, and the southerly track which *Titanic* was following, was 'about 50 miles'. The position of the iceberg about which the warning had been received 'was south of the northern track. I think there is more than 60 miles difference there', and 'to the northward of the southerly track'. 'Do you recollect which track it was nearest to?', Pitman was asked. 'I do not, sir', he replied.[3] In retrospect, of course, it is clear that *Titanic* and the iceberg were on a collision course!

What was *Titanic*'s course, before she struck, Hichens was asked. 'The course was north 70 west, sir', he replied.[4]

What made the passengers and crew suspect that something was amiss?
When *Titanic* struck, said Second Officer Lightoller, 'there was a slight shock and a grinding sound. That was all there was to it. There was no listing, no plunging, diving, or anything else'.[5] This suggests that it was *Titanic*'s hull which struck the iceberg, rather than her keel.

Lookout Frederick Fleet was asked whether 'there much of a jar to the ship' when *Titanic* struck. 'No, sir', he replied, 'just a slight grinding noise.'[6]

Lookout George T. M. Symons stated that he had taken his turn as lookout on the 8 p.m. to 10 p.m. watch. When *Titanic* struck, he was in his bunk. 'Was there much vibration to the ship', he was subsequently asked? 'No, sir; nothing to speak of, I thought', he replied. 'It was only a slight jar; a grinding noise.'[7] When *Titanic* struck, said Quartermaster George T. Rowe, he too 'felt a slight jar'.[8] Quartermaster Alfred Olliver stated that he 'was just entering the bridge' when 'the shock came' and he 'knew we had touched something. I found out we had struck an iceberg'.[9] Steward George Crowe was in bed but not asleep, he said, when at 'about 11.40 there was a kind of shaking of the ship and a little impact, from which I thought one of the propellers had been broken off'.[10]

Able Seaman Walter T. Brice stated that he had just left the seamen's mess room, when he 'heard a crash', which was 'like a heavy vibration. It was not a violent shock', and there was no jarring. The crash was followed by a 'rumbling noise', which continued for 'about 10 seconds'.[11]

When *Titanic* struck, said first class saloon Steward Frederick Dent Ray, he felt 'a kind of a movement that went backward and forward. I thought something had gone wrong in the engine room. I did not think of any iceberg'.[12]

UK Company Director Hugh Woolner was in the smoking room when the impact occurred. Said he, 'We felt a sort of stopping, a sort of, not exactly shock, but a sort of slowing down; and then we sort of felt a rip that gave a sort of a slight twist to the whole room'.[13]

When *Titanic* struck, said US Mechanical Engineer Norman C. Chambers, he was in bed. 'I noticed no very great shock', he said, 'the loudest noise by far being that of jangling chains whipping along the side of the ship'. US manufacturer George A. Harder and his wife Dorothy (née Annan) had retired for the night when, at 11.40 p.m. he said, 'I heard this thump. It was not a loud thump; just a dull thump. Then I could feel the boat quiver and could feel a sort of rumbling, scraping noise along the side of the boat'.[14] These two accounts strongly suggest a side-on collision of *Titanic* with the iceberg, rather than a grounding.

Said 21-year-old Daniel Buckley from Ireland, 'I wanted to come over here [to the USA] to make some money. I came in the *Titanic* because she was a new steamer. This night of the wreck I was sleeping in my room on the *Titanic*, in the steerage. There were three other boys from the same place sleeping in the same room with me. I heard some terrible noise, and I jumped out on the floor, and the first thing I knew my feet were getting wet; the water was just coming in slightly'.[15]

Said Mahala (née Dutton), wife of US businessman Walter D. Douglas, 'The shock of the collision was not great to us; the engines stopped, then went on for a few moments, then stopped again'.[16]

As to the sound, said Olliver, it 'was like she [*Titanic*] touched something; a long grinding sound, like', which 'did not last many seconds'.[17]

Evasive action by the crew
When 'three bells were struck', said Boxhall, 'that signifies something has been seen ahead'. He now 'heard the first officer [Murdoch] give the order 'Hard a starboard'. What did the order mean, he was asked. It was 'ordering the ship's head [forward portion] to port', he replied. 'Mr Murdoch followed on to say, 'I put her hard a starboard and run [ran] the engines full astern, but it was too close; she hit it".[18] In other words, *Titanic*'s engines had been put into reverse.

Given that *Titanic* was travelling at a speed of 21 knots, if the engines were reversed to full speed astern, what would her stopping distance have been? She would travel on 'about a quarter of a mile' before stopping, Lightoller replied, in a time of 'about a minute and a half, maximum'.[19] In other words, it would have made no difference to the outcome.

The sequence of events was as follows, said Lookout Reginald Lee. 'The helm must have been put either hard-a-starboard or very close to it' because *Titanic* 'veered to port, and it seemed almost as if she might clear it [the iceberg], but I suppose there was ice under water. As she struck on the starboard bow there was a certain amount of ice that came on board the ship. That was the forewell deck'[20] – i.e. the forward well deck. 'She started to go to port while I was at the telephone.' Had *Titanic* made a turn to port in order to swing the ship's bow away from the iceberg, Lee was asked? 'Yes; because we were making straight for it.'[21]

Titanic's location
At the time she struck, said Fifth Officer Lowe, *Titanic*'s position was 41° 46' north and 50° 13' west.[22]

The angle of impact

Did *Titanic* hit the iceberg 'squarely', Olliver was asked? 'No, sir; a glancing blow', he replied.[23] One day, proof would emerge that this was correct. When Lightoller arrived on deck, he noticed that the ship's speed 'was lessened' but that she was still 'apparently going slowly'. *Titanic* 'did not stop until she [had] passed the iceberg', said Lee.[24] This also indicates that the vessel struck a glancing blow.

What part of *Titanic* did the iceberg strike?

Looking down from the crow's nest, Fleet noticed that as *Titanic* was turning to port, 'the berg hit her on the starboard bow'.[25]

'It seemed to me to strike the bluff of the bow', said Boxhall, in reference to the iceberg, 'just where the ship begins to widen out on the starboard side'.[26]

Bluff: a bluff bow is broad and rounded (instead of being sharp).

Pitman declared that the iceberg 'had ripped the side of the ship out', the impact being on the starboard side. 'I should say halfway along the ship that her bottom was torn out, or at least her side, along the water.' By 'the side of the ship', said Pitman, he was referring to 'the bilge keel'. 'And that rendered the watertight compartments useless?' he was asked. 'In that part of the ship, yes', Pitman replied.[27]

Lee stated that *Titanic*'s contact with the iceberg was first made 'on the starboard bow, just before the foremast',[28] and 'about 20 feet' from the stem.[29] This was after the vessel had veered to port.

Foremast: located immediately above the 3rd Compartment (No. 2 Hold).

Lee deduced this by the fact that water was entering 'No. 1 or No. 2.' Hold of the ship, 'down in the firemen's quarters'.[30]

Titanic was 'ripped open' by the iceberg, said Lightoller. What was the extent of 'the ripping'? 'Nos. [Compartments, numbering from the bow] 1, 2, and 3, and the forepeak', he replied.[31] This was an inspired guess on Lightoller's part, but whether it was the truth or not remained to be seen.

Forepeak: the farthest compartment forward.

Subsequent action and events

When *Titanic* struck, said Ward, he 'got up' and 'went to the port [porthole] and opened it. It was very bitterly cold. I looked out and saw nothing. It was very dark'.[32]

Pitman was asked whether 'a failure of the watertight doors to work' was the reason why *Titanic* filled with water so quickly. No, he said, they were tested at Belfast, and he had personally witnessed the test.[33] Boxhall stated that immediately after *Titanic* struck, the watertight doors, which were electrically operated from the bridge, were closed as he had personally seen Murdoch close them.[34]

Did Captain Smith 'seem to know what you had struck?', Boxhall was asked. 'No', he replied. 'Did Mr. Murdoch?' 'Mr Murdoch saw it when we struck it.' 'Did he say what it was?' 'Yes, sir. He said it was an iceberg.' Boxhall recalled the conversation between Captain Smith and First Officer Murdoch. 'What have we struck?', the captain enquired. 'We have struck an iceberg', Murdoch replied.[35] This implies that, despite all the warnings about ice and icebergs that he had received, the captain was genuinely surprised.

Olliver was on the bridge when he heard the order 'hard a port'. This was 'after we had struck the iceberg'. Where was the iceberg when the order was given? It 'was away up stern', he replied.[36] In other words, when the order was given, *Titanic* had already passed the iceberg.

First class passenger C. E. Henry Stengel was asked how long after the impact was it before *Titanic*'s engines were stopped? 'I should say two or three minutes', he replied, 'and then they started again just slightly'.[37]

It was within five minutes of the collision, said John Hardy, Chief Steward Second Class, that he was given the order to sound 'the alarm to put on lifebelts'.[38]

Harder dressed and went up on deck, by which time *Titanic* 'was listing quite a good deal on the starboard side', he said.[39] Chambers, who likewise came on deck, 'noted ... an unusual coldness of the air'.[40]

Approximately seven minutes after the impact, said First Class Bedroom Steward Henry S. Etches, he heard the boatswain shout 'Close watertight bulkhead doors'.[41] This is at variance with Boxhall's statement, that the doors were closed immediately after the collision.

By 'about 10 minutes or so after the shock [of collision]', said Saloon Steward William Ward, *Titanic* 'was slowing down, then, and almost stopping then, I suppose. It being so dark, I really could not tell'.[42]

'Within 15 or 20 minutes' of the collision with the iceberg, Captain Smith 'visited the wireless room and instructed the operator to get assistance, sending out the distress call, C. Q. D.'[43]

The sinking

Could Pitman, who survived the sinking, state the exact time when *Titanic* disappeared beneath the waves? '2.20 exactly, ship's time', he declared. I.e. 2.20 a.m. on Monday 15 April 1912. 'I took my watch out at the time she disappeared, and I said, 'It is 2.20', and the [lifeboat's] passengers around me heard it.'[44]

What if *Titanic* had collided head-on with the iceberg?

Leo Shubow served on ice patrol duty for a season on the U.S. Coast Guard ship *Tampa* in the late 1950s. In 1959, Shubow stated of icebergs, that some 'had low-lying ledges extending from their sides'.[45] Was it with such a ledge that *Titanic* collided?

If the impact had occurred 'bows on', Pitman was asked, would *Titanic* have survived? 'Certainly', he said.[46] Similarly, Wilding was asked whether, if *Titanic* had struck the iceberg 'stem on' – i.e. head-on – would the ship have been saved? 'I am quite sure she would', he replied. However, such an impact 'would have killed every fireman down in the firemen's quarters'. This was because the 'momentum of the ship would have crushed in the bows for 80 or perhaps 100 feet'[47] – i.e. up to and including Compartment No. 3.

Here, it should be pointed out that it is not known whether the ledge upon which *Titanic* had foundered extended towards the direction of the ship. If it did, the results would have been just as catastrophic. However, if such a conjectural ledge had protruded only a short distance from the body of the iceberg, *Titanic* would have grounded and been brought to a halt when the bows struck the above-water body of the iceberg. In that case, the vessel might well have remained afloat. On the other hand, if the shape of the underwater portion of the iceberg facing *Titanic* was simply a vertical continuation of the above-water portion, then perhaps fewer of the forward compartments would have been punctured and again, *Titanic* may not have sunk, although there would doubtless have been considerable damage to her bows. However, what shape the underwater portion of the iceberg was, and whether there were other underwater ledges protruding from it, can never be known for certain.

The significance of ice aboard *Titanic*

Did any ice from the iceberg fall onto the decks? 'Yes', said Fleet, 'some on the forecastle light and some on the weather deck'. 'How much?' 'Not much; only where she rubbed up against it.'[48]

Forecastle light: presumably skylight.

Weather deck: shelter deck or 'C' deck.

Lee also noticed that some ice from the iceberg had fallen onto 'the forewell deck',[49] as did Able Seaman Frank Osman. 'It looked as if there was a piece broken off after she struck', he said, 'and the ice fell on board. I went and picked up a piece of ice and took it down below in my sleeping room.'[50] Lookout George Symons also reported seeing ice on *Titanic*'s forecastle when he came on deck. It was 'on the starboard side'. 'Was there any quantity of it?' 'Not such a great quantity', he replied.[51]

When John Collins, Assistant Cook First Class Galley went up on deck, 'up forward', he saw that the deck was 'almost packed with ice on the starboard side. I could not say what deck it was; it was on the same deck we slept on. Coming from the funnels it would be C deck, I think'. Here, Collins was evidently referring to the forewell deck.[52]

The forewell deck was 45 feet above the waterline and 'C' deck was 50 feet above the waterline. The conclusion is, therefore, that the iceberg was considerably taller than 50 feet in height.

22

The Outcome of the Impact

The likely sequence of events
When *Titanic* collided with the iceberg, the starboard portion the forward part of her hull was severely damaged, align water to enter the forward compartments of the ship. But where exactly was the damage, and of what severity was it? It would not be until the year 1997 that the answer would be revealed, as will be seen.

Captain Smith's response
'Were the engines reversed; was she backed?', Quartermaster Olliver was subsequently asked. 'After she struck', he replied, *Titanic* 'went half speed ahead'. 'Who gave the order?' 'The Captain telegraphed half speed ahead.' 'Did she have much way on [speed]', when 'he put the engines half speed ahead?' 'No, sir. I reckon the ship was almost stopped.'[1] Olliver concluded that what stopped *Titanic* was either 'hitting the iceberg', or the possibility that Captain Smith had 'backed the engines' – i.e. ordered them to be put into reverse.[2] In view of the lack of time available, the former seems the most likely scenario.

The impact, and how the energy was dissipated
Inertia is defined as the tendency to remain unchanged, or in physics, the property of matter by which it continues in its existing state of rest, or uniform motion in a straight line, unless that state is changed by an external force.[3]

The mass of the iceberg with which *Titanic* collided, 90% of which lay beneath the waterline, is estimated at about one billion tons, whereas the displacement of *Titanic* was 52,310 tons. In other words, the iceberg weighed in excess of 16,000 times the weight of *Titanic*.

Because of the solid nature of the ice, which had been compacted over many millennia by the time it parted from the glacier, *Titanic* was virtually running into a granite-hard, immovable object. And although steel, of which

Titanic was constructed, has five times the strength if ice, *Titanic* was not a solid mass of steel, but rather a hollow shell. Therefore, the effect of the ship impacting with the iceberg is akin to a hen's egg being dropped onto a marble floor!

The potential energy (that which a body possesses by virtue of it being in motion) released by the impact would probably not have caused the iceberg to move to any measurable extent. Instead, it was dissipated in destroying the structure of *Titanic*'s keel, disrupting the architecture of the hollow between the inner and outer hull, and distorting and fracturing the metal plates of which the hull was composed. This caused the rivets to fail, thus permitting the ingress of water.

Buoyancy

Samuel Halpern made a study of the effects of the ingress of water into the forward compartments of the *Titanic*. The bulwarks and the compartments are numbered 1,2,3,4 etc from forward to aft, there being 15 bulwarks in all.

Halpern began by defining the Apparent Flotation Pivot Point (AFPP), which is the hypothetical horizontal transverse axis on which ship pivots in the event of an imbalance of weight at either end. *Titanic*'s AFPP was located on her original waterline and approximately one third of the vessel's length from the stern. (And even as more and more water entered the forward part of the ship, the location of the AFPP would have remained in approximately the same location.)

Archimedes' principle, enunciated by the eponymous 3rd Century BCE Greek mathematician, states that a vessel totally or partially immersed in a fluid is subject to an upward force equal in magnitude to the weight of fluid it displaces. In the case of *Titanic*, the displacement was 52,310 tons. If a ship takes on water, and that water is equally distributed along its length, it will sit lower in the water (according to the amount of water taken onboard) but remain in its original horizontal position. However, if the water is contained solely in the front of the ship because less water has been displaced forward, the bows will sink lower in the water, the upward force being that much less. Also, because the ship has now pivoted around the AFPP, there will be a tendency of the stern to rise up – which is exactly what happened in the case of *Titanic*.

The angle of trim is defined as the angle between the original waterline, and the subsequent waterline after the flooding of various compartments in the ship. In the case of *Titanic*, for example, at 2:15 a.m. on 15 April 1912 when Second Officer Lightoller leapt into the water, the crow's nest was at sea level and the sea was engulfing the roof of the wheelhouse. 'From this description' said Halpern, 'we find the ship was about 10° down by the head' – i.e. the angle of trim was -10°.[4]

Wilding was asked how long, in the eventuality of the first five compartments being flooded, could such a vessel as *Titanic* be expected to remain afloat for. 'Probably for an hour – perhaps a little more', he replied. This was assuming that the watertight doors of the bulkheads had been closed. UK Day 19. In fact, *Titanic* had remained afloat for almost three hours, and not only that, evidence points to the fact that *not five but seven forward compartments were flooded*, as will be seen.

23

Survival! The Inadequately Filled Lifeboats

When *Titanic* set sail on her maiden voyage in April 1912, she carried insufficient lifeboats to accommodate her entire complement of passengers and crew. *Titanic* had 20 lifeboats, that could accommodate 1,178 people, or just over half of the total number on board, which was 1,317 passengers and 891 crew, total number 2,208.[1]

Recommendations to the UK government as to how many lifeboats a passenger liner should carry were the responsibility of the UK's Board of Trade (government department concerned with commerce and industry). So, was the Board of Trade negligent in this regard? In fact, the situation was more nuanced, and the Board of Trade's members had given the matter a great deal of thought when it came to the necessity of preserving lives at sea, as will now become clear.

In March 1886, 'the Board appointed a Departmental Committee consisting of three of their principal officers to inquire into the question of boats, rafts and life-saving apparatus carried by seagoing merchant ships'. Furthermore, 'speaking with special reference to passenger steam vessels carrying emigrants across the Atlantic to ports on the east coast of North America' – which was the case in respect of *Titanic* two decades later – 'The boat accommodation these vessels are forced to carry when sailing with emigrants is regulated by the scale in the Passengers Act, 1855, which provides for boat accommodation for 216 people as a maximum'.

However, the Board acknowledged 'that the boats carried by this class of vessel are also quite inadequate as an effectual means of saving life should a disaster happen to a ship with her full complement of passengers on board'. However, 'We are glad to be able to say that there are many liberal and careful shipowners who do all in their power to provide for the safety of their passengers by equipping their vessels with boats far in excess of the number required by statute'. *Titanic* was among that number. Conversely, however, 'there are others carrying large numbers of emigrants who do no more than they are required to do by law'.

The final conclusion of the Board was as follows: that the number of lifeboats 'required by the Act should be increased [by] 100 per cent, and in addition to them, that the owners should be induced to carry sufficient collapsible boats and approved rafts, so that each ship shall have sufficient life-saving gear for all on board at any one time …'.

The Merchant Shipping Act of 1888 was duly repealed, and the new Act came into operation on 1 June 1894. Under the Act, 'a table showing the minimum number of boats to be placed under davits, and their minimum cubic contents was issued by the Board'. It stipulated that the number of lifeboats to be carried should be determined by the tonnage of the vessel in question, and not by the number of passengers and crew carried. This, of course, was a totally nonsensical ruling! Furthermore, the table 'stopped short at the point where the gross tonnage of the vessels reached '10,000 and upwards'. Finally, 'the minimum number of boats under davits was fixed by the table at 16', whatever their tonnage might be.

From 1894 onwards, some dozen or so Atlantic liners of over 10,000 tons were built, not only in the UK but also in France, Germany, and the USA, 'culminating in the *Titanic* with a gross tonnage of 46,328'. However, 'the Rules and Table remained stationary, and nothing was done to them by way of change'.

So why this long delay, from 1894 to 1912? According to Sir Alfred Chalmers, Nautical Advisor to the Board of Trade from 1896 to August 1911, there were several reasons for this.

Travel by ocean going steamer was 'the safest mode of travel in the world', and this was all the more so because 'stronger and better ships, both from the point of view of watertight compartments and also absolute strength' were increasingly the norm. Second Officer Lightoller begged to differ. 'Had it been, for instance, the old *Majestic* or even the *Oceanic*', he said:

> 'the chances are that either of them would have been strong enough to take the blow and be bodily thrown off without serious damage. For instance, coming alongside with the old *Majestic*, it was no uncommon thing for her to hit a knuckle of the wharf a good healthy bump, but beyond, perhaps, scraping off the paint, no damage was ever done. The same, to a lesser extent, with the *Oceanic*'.

'Then ships grew in size, out of all proportion to their strength, till one would see a modern liner brought with all the skill and care possible, fall slowly, and ever so gently on a knuckle, to bend and dent a plate like a piece of tin.'

'That is exactly what happened to the *Titanic*. She just bump, bump, bumped along the berg, holing herself each time, till she was taking water in no less than six compartments, though, unfortunately we were not to know this until much later.'[2]

Furthermore, Chalmers 'considered from his experience' that 16 or more lifeboats 'was the maximum number that could be rapidly dealt with at sea and that could be safely housed without encumbering the vessel's decks unduly'. The routes to be taken across the oceans, which had been 'agreed upon by the different companies … tended to lessen the risk of collision, and to avoid ice and fog'. How ironic these words seem, bearing in mind what was shortly to befall *Titanic*!

Another factor in Chalmers's calculation was that many modern liners had now been fitted with wireless telegraphy, which meant that information about hazards could be shared, and help summoned if necessary. Chalmers also pointed out that lifeboats require manpower, and the more lifeboats there are, the more manpower is required. Finally, because ship owners were voluntarily carrying a complement of lifeboats over and above that required by the Act, Chalmers believed that 'any State Department [i.e. Department of the State] should hold its hand [delay] before it steps in to make a hard-and-fast scale for that particular type of shipping'.[3] Concern was, however, expressed for the design, integrity, and serviceability of existing lifeboats.

As *Titanic* was sinking, Captain Smith – to his credit – and his officers supervised the filling of the lifeboats. The number of lifeboats launched, and those responsible for their launching, is as follows:

On the port side:
Captain Smith, Wilde (Chief Officer),
    Lightoller (Second Officer)   1
Wilde, Lightoller   2
Wilde, Lightoller, Lowe   1
Wilde, Smith   1

Murdoch (First Officer)	1
Lightoller	3
Moody (Sixth Officer)	1
Total	10
On the starboard side:	
Wilde	1
Murdoch	2
Murdoch, Lowe	3
Moody	3
Pitman (Third Officer)	1
Total	10[4]

A total of only 716 persons were rescued from the lifeboats by the *Carpathia*,[5] the reason being that many of the lifeboats had been launched with far fewer passengers than they were designed to carry. Therefore, had the lifeboats been filled to capacity, another 462 souls could have been saved. (These figures are an approximation, as several died in the lifeboats having been rescued.) Why were the lifeboats not filled to capacity? After all, the rule of the sea is 'Women and Children *First*', not 'Women and Children *Only*'! Lightoller gave a possible explanation:

> 'I got just on forty people into No. 4 Boat and gave the order to 'lower away' and for the boat to 'go up to the gangway door' with the idea of filling each boat as it became afloat, to its full capacity. At the same time, I told the Bosun's Mate to take six hands and open the port lower-deck gangway door, which was abreast of No. 2 Hatch. He took his men and proceeded to carry out the order, but neither he nor the men were seen again. One can only suppose that they gave their lives endeavouring to carry out this order, probably they were trapped in the alleyway by a rush of water, but by this time the fo'c'sle head was within about ten feet of the water.'[6]

Lightoller implied that it was unsafe to fill the lifeboats completely with passengers before each bloat had been lowered at least part way towards the surface of the water. Mrs Ella White agreed with him. *Titanic*, she said, 'had no open decks except the top deck. How could they fill the lifeboats properly? They could not lower a lifeboat 70 feet with any degree of safety with more than 20 people in it. Where were they going to get any more in them on the way down?'[7]

A measure of peoples' desperation to get aboard the lifeboats was revealed by Saloon Steward George Crowe, who stated that some of the passengers, 'probably Italians or some foreign nationality other than English or American … attempted to rush the [life] boats'. Whereupon 'the officers threatened to shoot any man who put his foot into the boat'. Referring, evidently, to Fifth Officer Harold Lowe, Crow continued, 'he fired the revolver, but either downward or upward, not shooting at any of the passengers at all and not injuring anybody. He fired perfectly clear, upward or downward'. Was there any 'disorder after that?' 'No disorder', Crowe replied.[8]

24

The Ice Field into which *Titanic* had Sailed

Some idea of the extent and magnitude of the ice field into which Captain Smith had so blithely sailed the *Titanic* at almost full speed is illustrated by the following accounts.

At daybreak on the morning of Monday 15 April 1912, said Third Officer Pitman, when he was in a lifeboat and awaiting rescue, 'there were numerous bergs around me, maybe half a dozen', and he estimated that some of them towered as much as '100 feet or 150 feet' above the water.[1]

From the time he survived the sinking of *Titanic*, until daybreak, Fourth Officer Boxhall was asked, did he see any icebergs? 'No, sir; but I know that they were there', he replied. 'I saw nothing; but I heard the water [lapping] on the ice as soon as the lights went out on the ship. I heard the water rumbling or breaking on the ice. Then I knew that there was a lot of ice about; but I could not see it from the [life] boat'.[2]

But did Boxhall see any icebergs once he had been rescued by the *Carpathia*? Yes, he replied. On the morning of Monday 15 April 1912, when 'it was just breaking daylight', *Carpathia* 'seemed to have stopped within half a mile or quarter of a mile of the berg'. He saw as many as six icebergs and, he said, and he 'could see field ice then as far as the eye could see'. How did they appear to him? 'At daybreak they looked quite black', he replied, but 'after the sun got up, they looked white'.[3]

At daybreak on the Monday morning, said Fifth Officer Lowe, he saw 'quite a few' icebergs. 'I did not count them, but I should say anywhere up to 20.' How close was *Titanic* to the icebergs? 'I should say 4 to 5 miles.' 'In what direction?' 'All around.' Were they 'in the course' that *Titanic* was steering before she struck? 'Well, yes; they must have been in her way if they were all along the horizon.' Lowe was asked to estimate the size of these icebergs. 'I should say that the largest one was about, say, 100 feet high above water', he said.[4]

At daybreak on the Monday, said Quartermaster Hichens, 'we could see icebergs everywhere; also, a field of ice about 20 to 30 miles long, which it

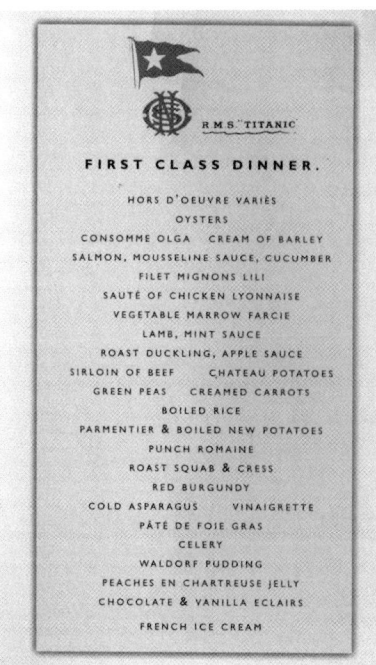

RMS *Titanic* beginning of day of sea trials, 2 April 1912. (*National Archives*)

RMS *TITANIC*

FIRST CLASS DINNER.

HORS D'OEUVRE VARIÈS
OYSTERS
CONSOMMÉ OLGA   CREAM OF BARLEY
SALMON, MOUSSELINE SAUCE, CUCUMBER
FILET MIGNONS LILI
SAUTÉ OF CHICKEN LYONNAISE
VEGETABLE MARROW FARCIE
LAMB, MINT SAUCE
ROAST DUCKLING, APPLE SAUCE
SIRLOIN OF BEEF   CHATEAU POTATOES
GREEN PEAS   CREAMED CARROTS
BOILED RICE
PARMENTIER & BOILED NEW POTATOES
PUNCH ROMAINE
ROAST SQUAB & CRESS
RED BURGUNDY
COLD ASPARAGUS   VINAIGRETTE
PÂTÉ DE FOIE GRAS
CELERY
WALDORF PUDDING
PEACHES EN CHARTREUSE JELLY
CHOCOLATE & VANILLA ECLAIRS
FRENCH ICE CREAM

RMS *Titanic*: First Class dinner menu. (The Titanic Pocket Book)

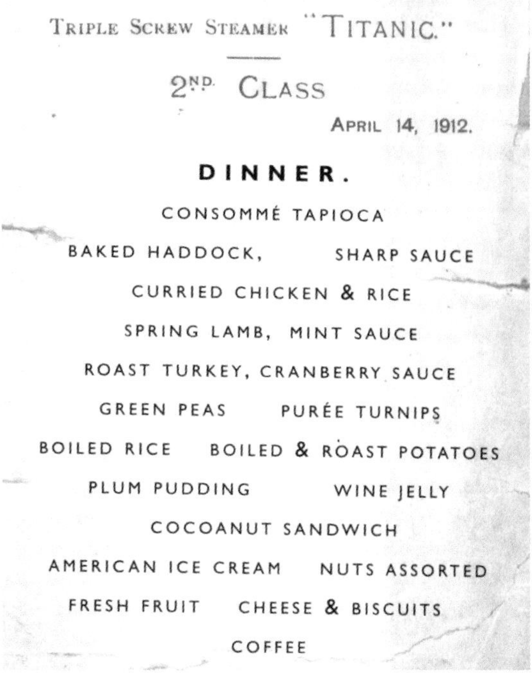

TRIPLE SCREW STEAMER "TITANIC."

2ND. CLASS

APRIL 14, 1912.

DINNER.

CONSOMMÉ TAPIOCA
BAKED HADDOCK,   SHARP SAUCE
CURRIED CHICKEN & RICE
SPRING LAMB, MINT SAUCE
ROAST TURKEY, CRANBERRY SAUCE
GREEN PEAS   PURÉE TURNIPS
BOILED RICE   BOILED & ROAST POTATOES
PLUM PUDDING   WINE JELLY
COCOANUT SANDWICH
AMERICAN ICE CREAM   NUTS ASSORTED
FRESH FRUIT   CHEESE & BISCUITS
COFFEE

RMS *Titanic*: Second Class dinner menu. (The Titanic Pocket Book)

Captain Smith aboard *Olympic* with his Irish wolfhound 'Ben'. Ben did not sail with his master aboard *Titanic*. (*SeaCity Museum, Southampton*)

As *Titanic* entered Southampton water on 10 April 1912, she caused a powerful wash to occur both ahead and behind her, causing the smaller ocean liner SS *New York* to be wrenched from her moorings. (*SeaCity Museum, Southampton*)

~Ship's Officers~

Captain, E. J. Smith, R.D. (Commr. R.N.R.) ~ *Captain*
Lt. Henry Tingle Wilde, R.N.R ~ *Chief Officer*
Lt. William McMaster Murdoch, R.N.R ~ *First Officer*
Sub-Lt. Charles Herbert Lightoller, R.N.R ~ *Second Officer*
Mr Herbert John Pitman ~ *Third Officer*
Sub-Lt. Joseph Groves Boxhall, R.N.R ~ *Fourth Officer*
Sub-Lt. Harold Godfrey Lowe, R.N.R ~ *Fifth Officer*
Mr. Paul James Moody ~ *Sixth Officer*

~Complement~

Mr. W. F. N. O'Loughlin ~ *Surgeon*
Mr. J. E. Simpson ~ *Asst. Surgeon*
Mr. H. W. McElroy ~ *Purser*
Mr. R. L. Barker ~ *Asst. Purser*
Mr. A. A. Ashcroft ~ *Clerk*
Mr. E. W. King ~ *Clerk*
Mr. J. R. Rice ~ *Clerk*
Mr. D. S. Campbell ~ *Third Class Clerk*
Mr. J. G. Phillips ~ *Telegraphist*
Mr. H. S. Bride ~ *Asst. Telegraphist*
Mr. A. L. Latimer ~ *Chief Steward*
Mr. J. T. Hardy ~ *Chief Second Class Steward*
Mr. J. W. Kieran ~ *Chief Third Class Steward*
Mr. J. A. Paintin ~ *Captain's Steward*
Mr. T. W. McCawley ~ *Gymnasium Steward*
Mr. F. Wright ~ *Squash Court Steward*

RMS *Titanic*: Officers and Complement. (The Titanic Pocket Book)

William M. Murdoch, First Officer of RMS *Titanic*.

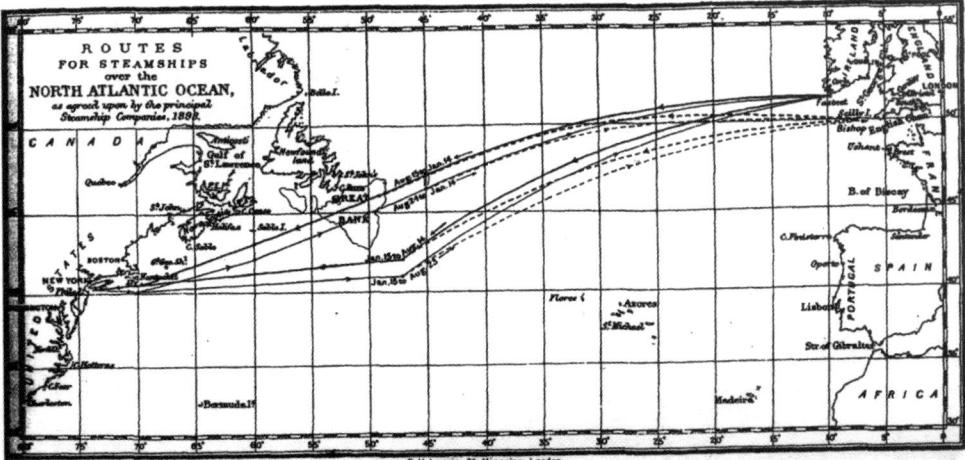

8 Routes 'Tracks') taken by White Star Liners to and fro across the Atlantic Ocean, August to January each year (to the north) and January to August each year (to the south, during the 'iceberg season'. *The Titanic Pocket Book.*

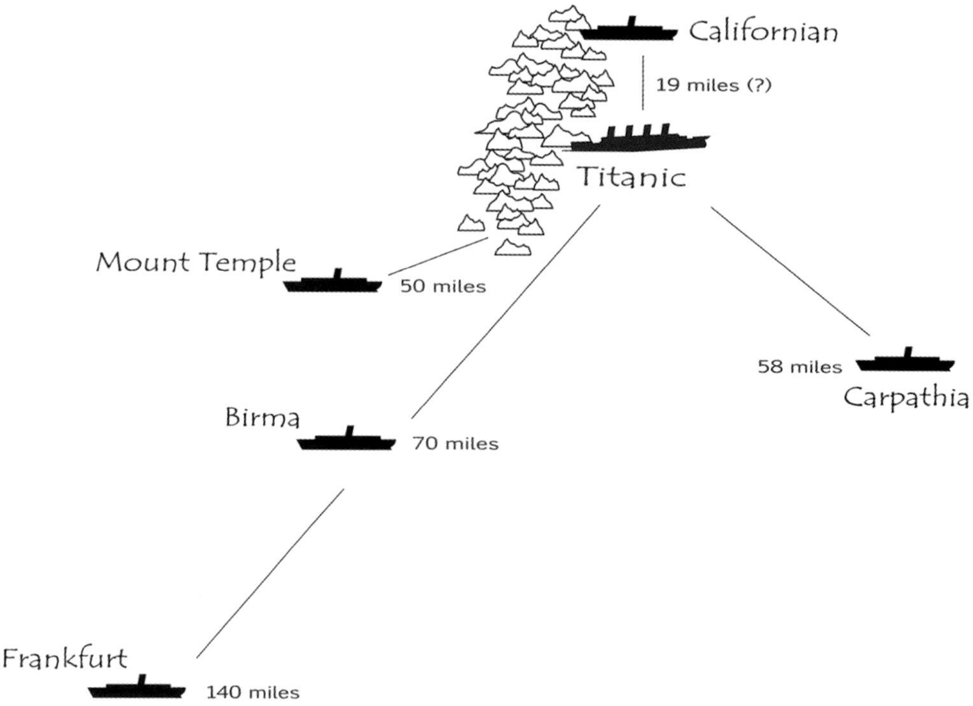

Ships in the vicinity of RMS *Titanic*, 14/15 April 1912.

Frederick Fleet, Lookout, RMS *Titanic*.

Reginald Robinson Lee c. 1900.

The running (navigation) light from RMS *Olympic*, which was identical to the one situated below the bridge on *Titanic*. (*SeaCity Museum, Southampton: Mike Cooper*)

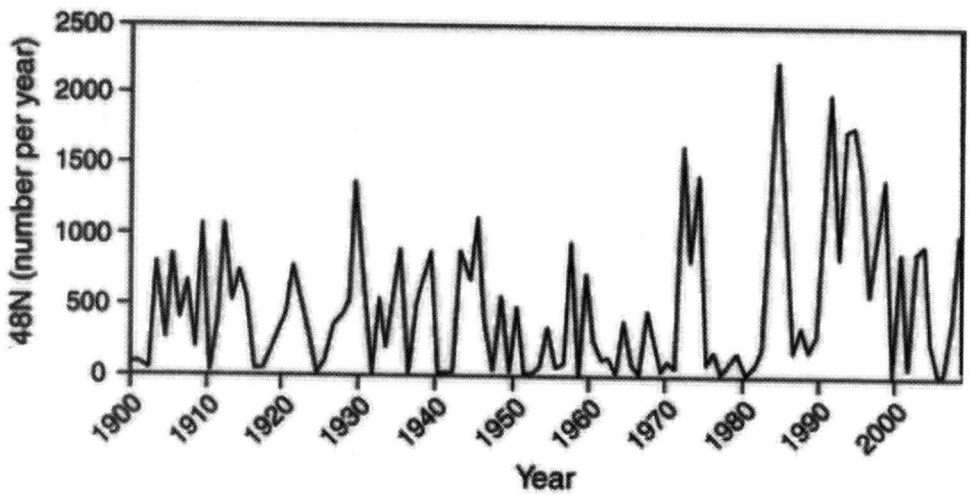

Total number of icebergs crossing latitude 48°N from north to south each year since 1900. (*Bigg, Grant R. and David J. Wilton*)

RMS *Titanic*: Lifeboat Number 6, on the morning of 15 April 1912, photograph taken by J. W. Barker, a passenger on the *Carpathia*. (*US National Archives*)

Arthur Henry Rostron,
Captain of RMS *Carpathia*.

The four surviving officers of RMS *Titanic* (left to right) Fifth Officer Harold G. Lowe, Second Officer Charles H. Lightoller, Fourth Officer Joseph G. Boxall, Third Officer Herbert J. Pitman (sitting), 1912.

The Hart family: father, Benjamin (who did not survive); daughter, Eva; and mother, Esther, circa 1910.

Thirteen of the 20 stewardesses who survived, Plymouth Docks. (*SeaCity Museum, Southampton*)

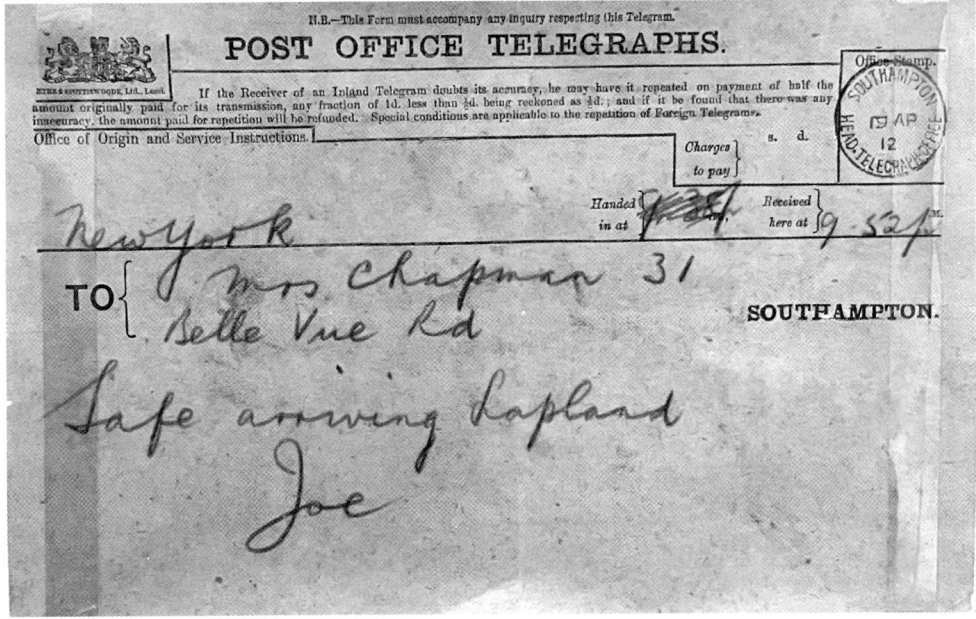

The Goodwin family from the UK, all of whom perished. *The Daily Mirror*, 26 April 1912.

Telegram sent to Ethel Chapman of 31 Belle View Road, Southampton, to say that her husband Joseph Charles Chapman had survived and was shortly to arrive in Lapland. (*SeaCity Museum, Southampton*)

The demise of *Titan*, from Morgan Robertson's novella *Futility*.

Impression of the iceberg with which *Titanic* collided: acrylic painting by UK artist Jenny Hare, from the photograph taken by Bernice Palmer. (*Smithsonian Institute, Washington DC*)

Guglielmo Marconi, 1909.

Edward John Smith, Captain of RMS *Titanic*, *New York Times*, published after his death on 15 April 1912.

Statue of Commander Edward J. Smith by Kathleen Scott, Beacon Park, Lichfield, Staffordshire, unveiled 29 July 1914.

Howard M. Buzzell, baby Howard (junior), and Laura Buzzell (née Cribb) Howard's wife. (*Photo: Hester Cribb*)

Howard M. Buzzell, with caption 'Two good Fellers' in Laura his wife's handwriting. (*Photo: Hester Cribb*)

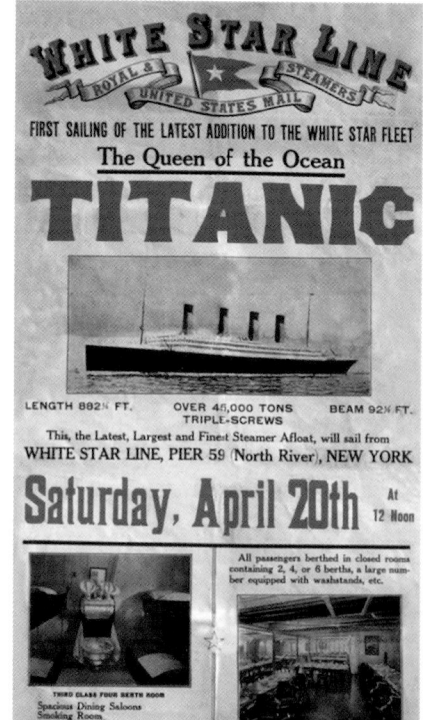

Advertisements for The White Star Line.
(*Wikimedia Commons*)

took the *Carpathia* 2 miles to get clear from when it picked the boats up. The icebergs was [were] up on every point of the compass, almost'.[5]

When the day broke, Fireman William H. Taylor was asked, how many icebergs did he see? 'We saw four', he replied.[6] In the morning, said Able Seaman George Moore, i.e. when it was light, 'there was ice all around'.[7] When daylight came, said John Hardy, Chief Steward Second Class, 'I should think there was, in my judgment, 5 or 6 miles of field ice, and any number of bergs. I could see them from the *Carpathia*'.[8]

'After daybreak, but not before', said Saloon Steward William Ward, 'there was quite a big lot of field ice and several large icebergs in amongst the field that I saw, and there were two or three icebergs separated from the main body of the field there'.[9]

It was only after 'it became daylight', said Saloon Steward George F. Crowe, that he saw 'three very large bergs'.[10]

When daylight came, said Boatswain's Mate Albert Haines, he saw ice 'all around … and there was a big field of ice there, too'. How many icebergs were there? 'I could not say', he replied. 'There was a good few of them, sir. They were dotted all over the place.' The field of ice was 'miles long', and he estimated the number of icebergs at between '30 to 50'.[11]

When day dawned, said Woolner, he saw a 'great may icebergs', the nearest of which was several miles away from the wreckage of *Titanic*. The icebergs were 'of different colors as the sun struck them. Some looked white and some looked blue, and some sort of mauve, and others were dark gray'. There was 'one double-toothed one' that was about 100 feet high.[12]

Passenger C. E. Henry Stengel stated that on the Monday morning, his lifeboat 'landed down into the water', and 'as soon as we were afloat, you could see icebergs all around, because we thought they were sailing vessels at first, and began pulling this way, and then turning around and going the other way. They were in sight all along the horizon'. One of the icebergs in particular caught Stengel's attention. It was 'a very large one', he declared, 'which looked something like the Rock of Gibraltar; it was high at one point, and another point came up at the other end …' As far as he could judge, 'it was 250 feet high at the highest point'.[13]

It was only when he was rescued by the *Carpathia*, said Stengel, that he gained a good view of the ice. 'There was a floe [sheet of floating ice] there that I should think was about 5 miles long, and I should say it would take

20 minutes [sailing] by the *Carpathia* to get by that field ice. It was ice all covered with snow.' Asked about its height above the water, Stengel replied, 'I should judge not over 2 feet; 2 or 3 feet'.[14]

Said US first class passenger Mrs J. Stuart White, 'After we got aboard the *Carpathia*, we could see 13 icebergs and 45 miles of floating ice, distinctly, right around us in every direction'.[15]

These numerous statements from eyewitnesses confirm that Captain Smith had driven *Titanic* into an extensive ice field littered with icebergs, some of which were substantial in size.

Now came another crucial piece of information, which confirmed that before she struck, *Titanic* had entered the domain of the icy cold Labrador Current, harbinger of icebergs. Said Moore, 'I believe the ice we saw in the morning [of Monday 15 April] was to the northward of where the *Titanic* had gone down'. And was the ice 'slowly coming down' – i.e. moving southwards toward *Titanic*? 'Yes', he replied, 'there were lots of bergs around, and there was a great field of ice, I should say between 20 and 30 miles long'. Was this 'solid ice'? 'Yes. The stretch of ice was very low, but there were also big bergs.' 'Would it have been possible for a ship to make its way among that ice?' 'No, sir.' 'It would have had to avoid it altogether?' 'Yes, sir.'[16]

Once again, here is damning evidence that Captain Smith ignored the sudden drop in temperature which signified *Titanic*'s transition from the influence of the Gulf Stream to the influence of the Labrador current, the significance, and dangers of which he as a seasoned transatlantic sailor, ought to have been well aware of.

Bearing in mind that *Titanic*'s lifeboats were not filled to capacity when the ship sank, Bartlett was asked if he had 'considered whether it would be desirable to have printed in large letters any notices on each boat that would indicate to the officer in the event of a disaster that the boat was capable of carrying either 65, or 40, or 47 persons, as the case might be?' The Inquiry understood that in the case of *Titanic*, 'the lifeboats under davits – were to carry 65 persons, the d boats ['Collapsible D or Engelhardt Type Collapsible Raft] 40 and the collapsible boats 47 each'. Although this was the custom on other ships of the fleet, said Bartlett, he did not know whether such a procedure had been adopted in the case of *Titanic*.[17]

Bartlett's attention was drawn to the fact that on *Titanic*'s sister ship *Olympic*, 'a small plate stating the number the [life]boat will carry' was 'riveted on to the boat'. This, however, was not a Board of Trade requirement. However, *it was* a Board of Trade requirement 'that both rafts and buoyancy apparatus must be marked in such a way as to indicate plainly the number of adult persons for which they are deemed sufficient. Plates will be supplied by the Board of Trade to be screwed on to the woodwork of both rafts and buoyancy apparatus indicating this number'. Furthermore, 'No raft or buoyancy apparatus is to be regarded as finally approved until the marking plate has been affixed'.[18]

Stengel was asked how long after the impact was it before *Titanic*'s engines were stopped? 'I should say two or three minutes', he replied, 'and then they started again just slightly'.[19]

25

The Speed of *Titanic* on Impact with the Iceberg: Visibility at the Crucial Time: Time Available to React to the Presence of the Iceberg

The Speed of *Titanic*

It is untrue that *Titanic* was competing for the Blue Riband accolade, awarded for the fastest transatlantic crossing. This was 'because ship hull design at the time was such that any speed over 20 knots could only be achieved by logarithmically increasing the horsepower of the engines, with consequent cost increases in engine construction and coal consumption'.[1]

Third Officer Pitman stated that at between 7.30 p.m. and 7.40 p.m. on Monday 15 April, he and Second Officer Lightoller made observations which included the speed of the ship, which was measured at 'about 21+ knots per hour', according to 'the log and the revolutions'. 'Were you trying to reach 24 knots', Pitman was asked. No, he replied, 'We had not the coal to do it'. The faster a ship travels, the greater is the rate at which coal is used up.[2] It was put to Pitman that '75 revolutions would indicate that she was going about 21½ knots?' He agreed. 'Approximately, yes, Sir.' 'Do you know whether she went any faster than that on that trip?' 'No; I do not think so. She never exceeded 76 revolutions [75 according to Ismay] at any part of the trip.'[3]

Lookout Reginald Lee was asked if, at the time of *Titanic*'s collision with the iceberg, there 'any difference in the speed at which the vessel was travelling compared with the rest of the voyage'? No, he replied, 'she seemed to be going at the same rate all the way'.[4] This was not in fact the case. *Titanic*'s speed over the 24-hour period from noon on 13 April to noon on 14 April was 22.06 knots, whereas for the previous 24-hour period her speed had been only 20.91 knots.[5]

Visibility of the Iceberg

Whether an iceberg is visible depends on several factor, including its size, colour, distance away, amount of light falling on it and being reflected from it, and the acuity of the human eye.

When the iceberg 'passed by', said Lookout Lee, then 'through this haze … you could see she was white; one side of it seemed to be black, and the other side seemed to be white'. In other words, there was a degree of haze at about the time of the impact. 'When I had a look at it going astern it appeared to be white'. 'At that time the ship would be throwing some light upon it; there were lights on your own ship?' This was a possibility, said Lee: 'It might have been that'.[6]

Size and shape

At the UK Inquiry it was pointed out that the top of the iceberg must have been higher than 'the forecastle head – i.e. higher than 55 feet above sea level, because after the collision ice fell from it onto the forecastle'.[7] Lookout Lee agreed. Before *Titanic* veered to port, he said, he observed the iceberg from the starboard side of the crow's-nest. How tall was it? 'It was higher than the forecastle', i.e. higher than the 55 feet that the forecastle rose above the waterline.[8]

Lookout Frederick Fleet had stated that 'the berg was not as high as the crow's-nest', which was about 40 feet above the forecastle deck – i.e. about 95 feet above sea level.

The iceberg was 'about the height of the boat deck', said Quartermaster Olliver, or perhaps 'just a little higher – i.e. 60 feet above the waterline. It was almost alongside of the boat, sir. The top did not touch the side of the boat, but it was almost alongside of the boat'.

It was the following morning, said Osman, that he saw the iceberg. Was he sure that it was the one that *Titanic* had struck. 'Yes, sir; you could see it was the one, sir.' It was only about 100 yards from *Titanic* when he saw it.[9] Osman estimated that the iceberg towered '100 feet out of the water. It was round, and then had one big point sticking up on one side of it'.[10]

Immediately after the collision, said Quartermaster George Rowe, he saw the iceberg on the 'starboard side of the ship'. It was 'very close to the ship', he said, 'almost touching it'. How tall was the iceberg? 'Roughly, 100 feet', Rowe replied.[11]

When *Titanic* struck, said Alfred George Crawford, Bedroom Steward First Class, he 'was on B deck'. He 'went out from B deck, out to the promenade there', and 'saw the iceberg passing along the starboard side'. As to its size, he 'could not see the top because there was a deck above us'. Was it 'higher than B deck?' 'Oh, yes', Crawford replied, 'much higher'.[12]

When *Titanic* struck, said Window Cleaner William Harder, he 'went to the porthole' and 'saw this iceberg go by. The porthole was closed. The iceberg was, I should say, about 50 to 100 feet away. I should say it was about as high as the top deck of the boat'.[13]

From these observations it is likely that the height of the visible portion of the iceberg was between 60 feet and 100 feet above the waterline.

Colour

In daylight, 'when the sun shines on them', said Captain Lord of the *Californian*, icebergs 'usually show white'. At night, however, they looked 'not exactly black', but 'grayish' in colour.

The colour of the iceberg 'was apparently dark, like dirty ice', said Osman.[14] 'It was not white, as I expected to see an iceberg', said Olliver. 'It was a kind of a dark blue'.[15] Said Crawford, the iceberg 'looked like a large black object going alongside the ship'.[16] Rowe, however, described the colour of the iceberg as 'just like ordinary ice'.[17]

Over hundreds of years, the ice contained within a glacier becomes buried under fresh layers of ice and snow:

> 'These heavy layers press the air out of the deeper layers of ice. This not only removes much of the air, it also causes the ice to form large, dense crystals. When light hits these crystals, they absorb long wavelengths of light. At the same time, they scatter short-waved blue light, which makes the ice appear blue.'

Therefore, when an iceberg 'calves' – i.e. breaks away from the parent glacier, the new face revealed by the fracture will therefore appear blue (until it becomes snow covered, that is); whereas the remainder of the iceberg, being covered in snow, appears white. So why is snow so reflective? This is because of the great quantity of air trapped between the snowflakes. 'Air bubbles scatter all wavelengths of light, making the snow appear bright white.'[18]

From the above accounts, the majority opinion was that the colour of the iceberg was dark blue or black which, of course, would have made it far more difficult to see. However, in pitch darkness, with starlight as the only source of light, an iceberg will have a very different appearance to how it looks in daylight. A girl passenger on one of the rescue boats, who happened to possess a camera, was able to shed more light on the subject (please excuse the pun!), as will shortly be seen.

Distance away

'In 1925, Fred Zeusler of the United States Coast Guard was in charge of the International Ice Patrol. According to his research, a medium-sized iceberg can be seen a nautical mile [1.15 land miles] away on a moonless, dark but clear night. On the night of the *Titanic* disaster in 1912, Halpern said, the sea was calm and smooth. Therefore, an iceberg could not be seen from the break of the waves. The only light that could have come from an iceberg would have been reflected starlight.'[19]

In 1959, Leo Shubow's book, entitled *Iceberg Dead Ahead!* was published. The most interesting item in this book, in respect of *Titanic*, is an experiment performed on board to determine how far away ice could be seen.

It was discovered that with excellent visibility and a clear sky, the furthest distance at which an iceberg could be seen was 36 miles. The usual distance was 12 to 20 miles; in haze, nine miles; in light fog and rain, one mile. On a clear, moonlit night, an iceberg could be seen two miles away, but on a clear moonless night only half a mile away.[20]

Amount of light falling on the iceberg, and being reflected from it

Influence of sun and moon

The visibility of an object to the human eye is dependent on the amount of light falling upon it. No light, and it is invisible. So where exactly were the sun and the moon at 11.40 p.m. on that fateful evening of Sunday 14 April 1912, when the iceberg was spotted?

Information kindly provided by the Royal Astronomical Society of Canada indicates the following. Under the heading 'Visibility of Celestial Bodies for the Night of April 14th 1912 to April 15th 1912, Standard Time' – i.e. local time – at the time of the impact the sun had set and was at an angle of -35°

below the horizon (whereas its lowest trajectory was -40°); whereas is the moon had also set and was at an angle of -35° below the horizon (whereas its lowest trajectory was -60°).[21]

Influence of airglow
Said Halpern, 'the light produced at sea on a typical moonless night has been estimated at being equal to the light of a single candle at the height of 180 feet. The big majority of this is produced by the phenomenon of airglow, which is the general dim light produced in the upper atmosphere by the action of solar radiation. In 1912, even the airglow was limited, the sunspot cycle then being at a minimum. With twilight long gone, *Titanic* was steaming into darkness with only the light of the stars, plus a little airglow that was available'.[22]

Airglow: a glow in the night sky caused by radiation from the upper atmosphere.[23]

Sunspot: a spot or patch that appears from time to time on the sun's surface, appearing dark by contrast to its surroundings.[24]

Influence of *Titanic*'s navigation lights
Titanic carried four electric powered navigation lights: 'a masthead light mounted on the foremast, red [for port] and green [for starboard] side lights under the wing cabs on the outside of the fore bridge, and a stern light on the outside of the rail out onto the poop'. *Titanic*'s masthead light was equivalent to 'a typical 40-watt incandescent bulb of today'. However, this was magnified about 25 times by the dioptric lens (which bends light by refraction, thereby increasing the power of the light) incorporated in it. However, none of these lights were powerful enough to have illuminated the iceberg, let alone to have been reflected by it.[25]

Only when the iceberg had passed by the side of the ship and it was illuminated by lights from the cabins, etcetera., did it become clearly visible.

Influence of the stars
There are three possible ways in which *Titanic*'s lookouts, or those on the bridge, could have become aware of an iceberg on a dark but starry night.

One is if the iceberg was gradually obscuring the view of the stars on the distant horizon as the ship approached it. However, this would have been more apparent at sea level, rather than on the bridge or even higher up on the crow' nest; or if the iceberg had become visible by virtue of the amount of starlight that was falling upon it?

'Illumination below 0.1 lux (100,000 microlux) is practically invisible to the human eye, and this falls in the so-called 'Scotopic' vision area.'[26]

Lux, the SI unit of illuminance, equal to one lumen per square metre.[27]

Illuminance: the amount of luminous flux per unit area.[28]

Luminous: giving off light.[29]

Scotopic: relating to or denoting vision in dim light, believed to involve chiefly the rods of the retina.[30]

However, on a starlit, clear, moonless night, excluding air glow the lux factor is 10^{-4} (or 200 microlux).[31]

Therefore, on the night in question, the iceberg would not have been visible to the naked eye simply by virtue of it being illuminated by starlight, because this would have been below the threshold of human vision. However, this is not the end of the story.

Ice is very reflective. As light waves strike an ice crystal they can be deflected and travel in a different direction. The Albedo value for ice is 0.6 to 0.9, in other words, most of the incident light is reflected.

Albedo: the proportion of the incident light that is reflected by a surface.[32]

It is possible that this is the way in which *Titanic*'s lookouts first became aware of the presence of the iceberg. (Starlight would also have been reflected off waves breaking on it, but that night the sea was calm.) However, it is perhaps more likely that the iceberg made its presence felt when it obscured the distance stars on the horizon.

Time to React

The question now is, how much time would the crew have had to react to the presence of the iceberg in *Titanic*'s path?

Shubow stated that, on a clear moonless night, an iceberg could be seen at a distance of half a mile away. Given that *Titanic* was travelling at a speed of 22½ knots (25.89 mph), this would have left insufficient time for her crew to react and slow the ship down to any meaningful degree. The vessel would therefore have travelled the half mile in a time of one minute 9.48 seconds, before striking the iceberg at a speed of almost 26 mph! In other words, the crew would only have had one minute 9.48 seconds to react to the emergency.

26

The Origin of Icebergs: Were Icebergs a One-off Phenomenon in 1912, at the Location in the Atlantic Ocean where *Titanic* Sank?

A glacier is formed when, after thousands of years of snowfall, the depth and weight of the snow causes compression, turning it into ice. Icebergs which reach the Grand Banks of Newfoundland, and its vicinity, are most likely to have originated from West Greenland, and in particular from the '20 major glaciers between the Jacobshaven and Humboldt Glaciers'.[1] An iceberg forms when a glacier splits and sheds a smaller mass of ice.

The progress of icebergs originating from Greenland's west coast is, however, not straightforward. First, the West Greenland Current carries it northwards to the north of Baffin Bay where it meets the Baffin Island Current. This carries it southwards down the east coast of Baffin Island and through the Davis Strait. Finally, it reaches the Labrador Sea where the Labrador Current takes it southwards down the east coast of Labrador and the east coast of Newfoundland.

Shubow asked US oceanographer and marine biologist Professor Henry B. Bigelow to explain more about the movement of icebergs. 'How long does it take for these bergs to come down the to the North Atlantic to strike the shipping lanes?' he enquired. 'Well, it may take about ten to twelve months', Bigelow replied. 'They travel at about one-half knot an hour and come by Cape Race, Newfoundland around the first of March. That's why the Ice Patrol usually begins sometime then, and continues through the danger months of April, May, June, and even July.'[2] The fact that April was regarded as one of the danger months is highly significant because it was in mid-April that *Titanic* struck the iceberg.

Fourth Officer Boxhall, who had served for five years on White Star liners, mainly on the transatlantic route, was asked to state how far east had he ever seen icebergs. 'It has been many years since I have seen any, until this time', he replied. 'Is it understood by mariners and navigators that they are more frequent in the latitude of the Grand Banks.' Was this true? Yes, Boxhall replied, 'around 50 [degrees] west; 47 to 50 west, I think, as near as I can remember'.

Grand Banks: a series of underwater plateaus south-east of the Island of Newfoundland.

In fact, the Grand Banks lie between latitude 48° to 43° North and longitude -54° to -45° West. *Titanic* sunk when she was at latitude 41° 43' 57.0" North and longitude -49° 56' and 48.8" West. The vessel was therefore well to the south of the Grand Banks at the time of the sinking.

And was it 'customary to be particularly careful in that vicinity?' 'Oh, yes, sir', said Boxhall.[3]

Was the year 1912 in any way unusual in respect of the iceberg risk to shipping? Said UK Professor of Earth System Science Grant R. Bigg and UK data scientist David J. Wilton:

> 'The year 1912 was indeed unusual, with 1,038 icebergs observed to cross 48°N. However, this number does not even reach the 90th percentile of the annual number distribution.' In fact, in 14 of the 112 years studied (1900 to 2012) the number of icebergs to cross 48° N exceeded this number.'

The authors therefore concluded that:

> '1912 was a year of raised iceberg hazard, but not exceptionally so in the long term. In the surrounding decades (1901–1920) there were 5 years with at least 700 icebergs crossing 48° N [the northernmost extremity of the Grand Banks], and 1909 recorded a slightly higher flux [outflowing of icebergs] than 1912.' 1912 was therefore 'a significant ice-year, but not extreme'.[4]

27

The Invidious Position of *Titanic*'s Lookouts: Absence of Searchlights; Absence of Binoculars; Absence of Goggles

Searchlights

Second Officer Lightoller was asked whether, in his opinion, 'a searchlight would be a benefit or a detriment on a ship'. In his opinion, it was 'detrimental to those on whom the light is shining, but beneficial to those who are behind the light'. 'In this case it would not have been detrimental to the iceberg, if it was an iceberg?', Senator Bourne remarked dryly. 'Certainly not', Lightoller agreed.[1]

If *Titanic* had been equipped with a searchlight and if this had been shone from the bow of the ship, could this have 'apprised the vessel of its proximity to you', Fourth Officer Boxhall was asked. Whereupon he gave a far more rational and plausible answer. 'Well, no doubt a searchlight might have called attention to it then', he replied.[2]

Navigation lights

Could *Titanic*'s navigation lights have illuminated the iceberg? The ship carried four electric navigation lights including: a masthead light mounted on the foremast; red and green sidelights under the wing cabs on the outside of the Navigating Bridge (red on the port side and green on the starboard side); a stern light on the outside of the rail of the poop deck.

Wing cabs: observation points on either side of the bridge, providing unobstructed views ahead and on either side.

> 'All the lights were equipped with dual filament bulbs' which 'more than met the minimum requirements regarding navigation lights that existed at the time. For example, *Titanic*'s electric masthead light generated 32 candlepower, which is equivalent to a 40-watt incandescent bulb today.

However, the dioptric lens in the masthead light [which served to focus the light] amplified the brightness of the bulb by about 25 times' – i.e. to 1,000 watts. 'Given its height above the waterline (142 feet), the light would have been visible on a clear, dark night from about 22 nautical miles away – the distance to the horizon – to someone standing on a ship's bridge, 45 feet above the water. The light would have appeared as bright as a magnitude 1.56 star.'[3]

Clearly, *Titanic*'s navigation lights were adequate to warn other shipping of her presence during the hours of darkness, but they were not designed to illuminate objects in her path, nor were they powerful enough to have done so.

Binoculars ('Glasses')

At the UK Inquiry the question was asked of Lookout Frederick Fleet, who had four years previous experience of being a lookout aboard the *Oceanic*, 'Do you think if you had had glasses, you could have seen the iceberg sooner?' 'Certainly', he replied. 'How much sooner do you think you could have seen it?' 'In time for the ship to get out of the way', he replied without hesitation. 'So that it is your view that if you had had glasses, it would have made all the difference between safety and disaster?' 'Yes.' Had binoculars been available to him in the crow's nest, would he have used them? 'Yes', Fleet replied. 'Constantly?' 'Yes.'[4] The question was again put to Fleet at the US Inquiry, if he had been issued with glasses, could he 'have seen this black object [the iceberg]' at 'a greater distance'. Again, he was in no doubt as to the answer. 'We could have seen it a bit sooner', he replied. 'How much sooner?' 'Well, [soon] enough to get out of the way.'[5]

Another advantage of binoculars was that they shielded the eyes of the lookouts from the unrelenting blast of freezing cold air that was blown into their faces by virtue of the speed of the ship through the water.

Was it possible 'to see better with your plain eyes than you can with artificial glasses', Lookout George A. Hogg was asked? With the aid of glasses, 'if you happen to see something on the horizon you can pick your ship out, if it is a ship, for instance', he replied. In other words, in daylight, binoculars were useful for identifying distant objects.[6] But what about in darkness, as on that fateful night of 14/15 April 1912? 'If we had had the glasses', said Hogg, 'we might have seen the berg before' – i.e. in time to avoid the collision.⁷ But how might this have been possible? Perhaps by observing starlight reflected by the snow-covered iceberg – after all, snow is an excellent reflector of light; or by noticing how the looming iceberg obscured the stars on the distant horizon.

Goggles

Italian photographer and optician Giuseppe Ratti, who worked for the family firm 'Berry' opticians, produced protective goggles for pilots of aircraft and for racing car drivers – 'two occupations that required maximum protection for the eyes with minimum interference to vision'. However, no such provision was made for ship's lookouts. In contrast, by the time of the Second World War, goggles were routinely supplied to sailors of the US (and other navies), in order 'to protect lookouts' eyes from wind and weather …'.⁸

28

Fate of the Captain, Passengers and Crew: Human Drama and Human Tragedy

Captain Smith did not survive the sinking and his body was never found. Of *Titanic*'s seven officers, three did not survive the sinking: Chief Officer Wilde; First Officer Murdoch; and Sixth Officer Moody.

All six of *Titanic*'s lookouts survived the sinking.

Human Drama

Every person aboard *Titanic* had their own story of human drama and human tragedy to tell, but of course, hundreds did not live to tell the tale.

As *Titanic* was sinking, Second Officer Lightoller was sucked into a ventilation shaft. However, he survived and scrambled aboard a life raft. Seconds later one of *Titanic*'s funnels collapsed into the sea, narrowly missing the raft.

It was 'a very distressing scene', said Woolner, to see 'the men parting from their wives'.[1] In fact, many wives chose to remain with their husbands, even though they knew that they were facing almost certain death.

When the sixth lifeboat was being prepared for launch, said 21-year-old steerage passenger Daniel Buckley, some passengers, sailors, and firemen, but no women, jumped into it. 'So, I said I would take my chance with them', he said. Whereupon two officers arrived with a group of steerage passengers. The men were ordered out of the lifeboat and their place was taken by the women from steerage. However, six men remained in the lifeboat. 'I think they were firemen and sailors', said Buckley. He himself also remained in the boat, thanks to the quick wittedness of one of the lady passengers. This woman, who Buckley believed was Lady Astor, threw her shawl over him. In fact, it was not Madeleine Astor (née Force), wife of Colonel John Jacob Astor IV, who was aged only 18 and 5 months pregnant, as she was in a different lifeboat. 'Then they did not see me, and the boat was lowered down into the water', Buckley continued, 'and we rowed away out from the steamer.'[2]

Did passengers in steerage have as good a chance of escaping from *Titanic* as the first and second class passengers had, Buckley was asked? Yes, he replied, but only after they had broken the gate that was keeping them in. After that, 'all the steerage passengers went up on the first class deck …. They all got up there. They could not keep them down'.[3]

As the first collapsible was being lowered on the starboard side, said first class passenger Hugh Woolner, 'there was a sort of scramble … and I looked around and I saw two flashes of a pistol in the air, and he heard Murdoch 'shouting out, "Get out of this, clear out of this", and that sort of thing, to a lot of men who were swarming into a boat on that side'.[4]

Whereupon Swedish businessman Mauritz B. Steffanson and I went up to help to clear that boat of the men who were climbing in', continued Woolner, 'because there was a bunch of women – I think Italians and foreigners – who were standing on the outside of the crowd, unable to make their way toward the side of the boat. So, we helped the officer to pull these men out, by their legs and anything we could get hold of'.[5]

Having gone to his allocated lifeboat and realized that there was 'no chance there', John Collins, Assistant Cook First Class Galley, ran to the saloon deck on the port side where he encountered a woman and her two children, one of whom was in the arms of a steward. Collins 'took the child off of the woman', who was crying, and made for the starboard side, where a collapsible boat was being launched. However, as *Titanic*'s bow was about to sink, he was told to go aft, where 'there was a boat getting launched'. But 'we were just turning around and making for the stern end when the wave washed us off the deck – washed us clear of it – and the child was washed out of my arms'. Collins stated that there were 'hundreds on the starboard side' who, like himself, had been swept into the sea.[6]

After *Titanic* had sunk, Moore was asked if his lifeboat had made 'any effort to go back' and 'attempt to rescue some of the people who were sinking'? 'No, sir', he replied. 'All the people in the boat wanted to get clear of the ship. They did not want to go near her. I do not think anybody could live much more than 10 minutes in that cold water. If we had gone back, we would only have had the boat swamped. Five or six pulling on that boat's gunwales would no doubt have capsized the boat.'[7]

Human tragedy

In her affidavit, first class passenger Mrs Emily Ryerson described how, when she was in the lifeboat and *Titanic* was sinking, 'someone called out, 'Pull for your lives, or you'll be sucked under', and everyone that could rowed like mad. I could see my younger daughter [Ellen] and [first class passengers Mrs [Marian L.] Thayer and Mrs [Madeleine T.] Astor rowing, but there seemed to be no suction. Then we turned to pick up some of those in the water. Six or seven men, principally stokers, stewards, sailors, etc' were rescued in this way. However, they 'were so chilled and frozen already they could hardly move. Two of them died in the stern later and many were raving and moaning and delirious most of the time'. The lifeboat had 'no lights or compass. There were several babies in the boat, but there was no milk or water'.[8]

The headline on the front page of the *Daily Mirror*'s edition of Friday 26 April 1912 read: 'Family of Eight, who were on the *Titanic* by Chance, All Drowned in the Disaster because there were Not Enough Lifeboats'. This was the Goodwin family of Kensington: Frederick Joseph Goodwin (father, aged 42); Augusta (mother, 43); Lilian Augusta (daughter, 16); Charles Edward (son, 14); William Frederick (son, 13); Jessie Allis Mary (daughter, 12); Harold Victor (son, 10), Sidney Leslic (son, 18 months). The family was en route to join Mr Goodwin's brother in Niagara, where they intended to settle.

When *Titanic* was sinking, said Moore, 'we were about a quarter of a mile away' in the lifeboat, 'and the cries [of the drowning who were in the water] did not last long'.[9]

Lookout Frank Evans stated that he was in Number 10 lifeboat, which was tied up to Number 12. Number 14 lifeboat now approached, commanded by *Titanic*'s fifth officer, Harold Lowe. Lowe ordered Evans to transfer to his lifeboat and to 'go over into the wreckage and pick up anyone that is alive there. So, we got into his boat and went straight over toward the wreckage. We picked up four men there, Sir; alive'. However, 'one died on the way back, Sir'. 'There were plenty of dead bodies about us', Evans continued. 'You couldn't hardly count them, sir. I was afraid to look over the sides because it might break my nerves down'. 'Did these bodies have life preservers on', he was asked? Yes, he replied, but despite this, 'they simply had perished, sir', he said.[10]

Gracie stated that he was adrift on a raft 'all night'. After *Titanic* had sunk, he saw 'wreckage', and 'bodies', and he heard 'the horrible sounds of drowning people and people gasping for breath'.[11]

Jacob William Gibbons was born at Charminster, Dorset, on 10 October 1875. Jacob, his father and namesake, was a farm labour and gardener at the Dorset Lunatic Asylum (subsequently the Herrison Hospital), whose wife was Kezia (née Gibbs). In 1898, Gibbons married Lottie Jane Puckett and a couple settled at Studland. They had five children.

On 4 April 1912, when Gibbons signed on for the *Titanic* as a second class steward, he and Lottie were proprietors of Harbour View, a lodging house in Studland. He recalled the night of the sinking of the great ship:

'The shock was very slight, and to this fact I attribute the great loss of life, as many of those abroad [i.e. who were awakened by the impact] must have gone to sleep again under the impression that nothing serious had happened. When I got up on deck the boats were being lowered away, but many of the passengers seem to prefer sticking to the ship. I helped some of the passengers into Boat No. 11, including two little children. We drew away from the *Titanic* in the charge of Mr [Joseph Thomas] Wheat, another steward [Assistant Second Steward], and when about half a mile away saw her sink. The cries of those on board were terrible, and I doubt whether the memory of them will ever leave [me] during my lifetime. It has been denied by many that the band was playing, but it was doing so, and the strains of 'Nearer My God to Thee' came clearly over the water, with a solemnity so awful that words cannot express it.'

On arrival at New York aboard the *Carpathia*, Gibbons sent a telegram to his family with the simple message: 'Saved, well, Daddy'.

Gibbons died on 27 February 1965, and his ashes were scattered in the cemetery of Studland's Wesleyan Church.[12]

Ethel (née Smith), the wife of Boots Steward Joseph Chapman of 31 Belle Vue Road, Southampton received the following telegram from her husband to say that he had survived. It read: 'Safe arriving Lapland Joe'. By contrast, Madge Sedunary (née Tizzard) of 34 Emsworth Road, Shirley, Southampton received a telegram to say that her husband Samuel Francis Sedunary, Third Class Steward, had perished. It read: 'Much regret Sedunary not saved'.

News of *Titanic*'s sinking was posted in the window of the *Southampton Times* newspaper at 11 a.m. on the morning of the sinking, 15 April 1912. As reports came in, handwritten lists of the survivors' names were posted up by the White Star Line company at their offices in Canute Road. At the same time telegrams began to arrive at Southampton, many bearing the fateful words 'NOT SAVED'.

Although the exact figure for the number of victims of the sinking is not known for certain, the US Inquiry gave the number as 1,517, whereas the UK Inquiry gave the number as 1,503.

Seven ships participated in retrieving the deceased from the sea, the bodies being numbered 1–335. They were:

CS *Mackay-Bennett*: US cable laying ship (Bodies No. 1–306).
CS *Minia*: cable repair ship, based in Halifax, Nova Scotia (Bodies No. 307–323). (Bodies No. 324 and 325 were not allocated.)
CGS *Montmagny*: Canadian government ship (Bodies No. 326–329).
SS *Algerine*: based in St John's, Newfoundland (Body No. 330).
RMS *Oceanic*: White Star ocean liner (Bodies No. 331–333).
SS *Ilford*: British cargo ship (Body No. 334).
SS *Ottawa*: UK ocean liner (Body No. 335),

Upon retrieval and having been identified as far as was possible, many of the bodies were buried at sea – for example, 6 from the *Carpathia*. Otherwise, the bodies of 209 identified and unidentified victims of the sinking were brought to Halifax, Nova Scotia, where 121 were buried in the non-denominational Fairview Lawn Cemetery, 19 in the Roman Catholic Mount Olivet Cemetery, and 10 in the Jewish Baron de Hirsch Cemetery. 59 bodies were repatriated.[13]

29

The Alleged Negligence of Captain Stanley Lord of the SS *Californian*

Proximity of other ships to *Titanic* when she was in distress
According to the US Senate Investigation, the distance in miles from *Titanic* of other vessels, when her various distress signals were being sent out were as follows:

Californian	19½
Mount Temple	49
Carpathia	58
Birma	70
Frankfurt	153
Virginian	170
Baltic	243
Olympic	512[1]

The *Californian*, therefore, at only about one hour's steaming time away, was in by far the best position to render assistance.

***Titanic*'s emergency rockets**
'The 1912 International Rules of the Road governing Signals of Distress are quite clear: Article 31: Class 1, called for – a cannon or explosive device [with report] fired at one-minute intervals. The device's report was the *sound* of distress.' Furthermore, 'Article 31: Class 3, covered the *sight* of distress which is a rocket of any color fired one at a time at short intervals.'[2]

Said John G. Gillespie, US co-author with his wife Vera of *The Titanic Man*, 'An explosion or report at one-minute intervals satisfies the sound signal requirement, and the white shower of stars at one-minute intervals satisfies the sight requirement'. Clearly therefore, when *Titanic* fired her rockets to indicate that she required urgent help, her crew had a duty to fire the rockets strictly at one-minute intervals, and this being the case, the exploding rockets would be instantly identifiable as international 'Signals of Distress'.

'If this procedure had been followed', Gillespie continued, then 'no one could ever question the meaning of the *Titanic*'s rockets'.

Commencing at 12:45 a.m. on the morning of Monday 15 April 1912, Fourth Officer Boxhall ordered one rocket to be fired. 'During the following hour or so, the *Titanic* fired an additional seven rockets – for a total of eight. The average time between rocket firings calculated to be seven to eight minutes. Even at four-minute intervals (as one witness mentioned), there were long periods of time when no rocket activity was seen.'[3]

This clearly shows either that *Titanic*'s crew failed to understand the correct procedure for the firing of her distress rockets or were unable to do so in the dire circumstances in which they found themselves.

Nonetheless, Second Officer Lightoller was incensed at the failure of Captain Lord of the *Californian* to render assistance. Having lowered the lifeboats, he said, he 'could see a steamer's steaming lights a couple of miles away on our port bow. If I could get the women and children into the boats, they would be perfectly safe in that smooth sea until the other ship picked them up, if the necessity arose'.

'At this time, we were firing rocket distress signals, which explode with the loud report a couple of hundred feet in the air. Every minute or two [but not every minute as prescribed] one of these went up, bursting overhead with a cascade of stars. 'Why were we firing these signals, if there was no danger', was the question, to which I replied that we were trying to call the attention of the ship nearby, as we could not get her with wireless. *That ship was the Californian.*' In fact, the identity of this vessel is a matter of doubt, as will be seen.

'The distress signals fired were seen by the officer of the watch on the *Californian*, also by several members of her crew. Even the flashes from our Morse lamp were seen but finally judged to be 'just the mast-head light flickering'.'

'To let pass [i.e. not be alert as to] the possibility of a ship calling by Morse, in the existing circumstances then surrounding her was bad enough; but to mistake, distress signals was inexcusable, and to ignore them, criminal. In point of fact, the O.O.W. [Officer of the Watch] alone saw and counted five distress signals (or, as he reported them to Captain Lord [of the *Californian*], 'five white rockets').'

Lord's response was to tell the officer to 'to go on Morsing', and if he received any further information to send it down to him'.

'It is an unqualified fact', Lightoller continued, 'that every single one of our distress signals – unmistakable and urgent calls for help, were clearly seen by the *Californian*. These signals are never made, except in cases of dire necessity. The O.O.W. of the *Californian* fully appreciated this fact as was evidenced by his remark to the Apprentice on watch with him, 'A ship is not going to fire rockets at sea for nothing'.'

'Shortly after counting eight 'rockets' he again sent down word to the Captain, with the added rider to the Apprentice, 'be sure to wake him and tell him that altogether we have seen eight of these white lights, like rockets, in the direction of this other steamer'.'

'Precisely at 2:40 a.m. this Officer of the watch again called Captain Lord, this time by voice pipe, and told him that the ship from which he had seen the rockets, had disappeared.'[4]

US *Titanic* survivor Colonel Archibald Gracie was equally appalled by Captain Lord's failure to respond. Said he, 'Our hopes were buoyed with the information, imparted through the ship's officers, that there had been an interchange of wireless messages with passing ships, one of which was certainly coming to our rescue. To reassure the ladies, of whom I had assumed special charge, I showed them a bright white light of what I took to be a ship about five miles off and which I felt sure was coming to our rescue'.

'The light, as I have since learned, with tearful regret for the lost who might have been saved, belonged to the steamer *Californian* of the Leyland Line.' Captained by Stanley Lord, she was 'bound from London to Boston. She belonged to the International Mercantile Marine Company, the owners of the *Titanic*. This was the ship from which two of the six "ice [warning] messages" were sent', the second of which stated that the SS *Californian* was 'stopped and surrounded by ice'. But was this ice sufficient to prevent the ship from moving? Both the UK and US Enquiries concluded that no, it was not, as will be seen.

Up until 11:30 p.m. on the previous evening of Sunday April 14th, Gracie continued, 'the wireless operator of SS *Californian* was listening with 'phones on his head, but at 11:30 p.m., while the *Titanic* was still talking to Cape

Race, the former ship's operator 'put the 'phones down, took off his clothes, and turned in'.'

Information 'which we learned after our arrival in New York', was 'that the Captain of the *Californian* and his crew were watching our lights from the deck of their ship, which remained approximately stationary until 5:15 a.m. on the following morning [15 April 1912]. During this interval it is shown that they were never distant more than six or seven miles. In fact, at 12 o'clock [midnight on 14/15 April] the SS *Californian* was only four or five miles off at the point and in the general direction, where she was seen by myself and at least a dozen others, who bore testimony before the American Committee [of Inquiry], from the decks of the *Titanic*'.

'The white rockets which we sent up … were also plainly seen at the time. Captain Lord was completely in possession of the knowledge that he was in proximity to a ship in distress. He could have put himself into immediate communication with us by wireless, had he desired confirmation of the name of the ship and the disaster which had befallen it. His indifference is made apparent by his orders to 'go on Morseing [Morsing]'.' This was 'Instead of utilising the more modern method of the inventive genius and gentlemen, Mr Marconi, which eventually saved us all.' i.e. by the exchanging of Marconigrams by wireless telegraphy.

"The ice by which the SS *Californian* was surrounded', concluded the UK Inquiry, 'was loose ice extending for a distance of not more than two or three miles in the direction of the *Titanic*. The night was clear, and the sea was smooth. When she first saw the rockets, the SS *Californian* could have pushed through the ice to the open water without any serious risk and so have come to the assistance of the *Titanic*'. Had she done so, Gracie concluded, 'she might have saved many if not all of the lives that were lost'.'[5]

In respect of the SS *Californian*, the US Inquiry was scathing in its verdict:

> 'Her officers and crew saw the distress signals of the *Titanic* and failed to respond to them in accordance with the dictates of humanity, international usage, and the requirements of law. The only reply to the distress signals was a counter signal from a large white light which was flashed for nearly two hours from the mast of the *Californian*. In our opinion such conduct, whether arising from indifference or gross

carelessness, is most reprehensible and places on upon the commander of the *Californian* a grave responsibility.'[6]

The UK Inquiry was equally scathing, stating that the SS *Californian* 'could have reached the *Titanic* if she had made the attempt when she saw the first rocket. She made no attempt'.[7]

Halpern had some interesting and useful comments to make about the matter. It was at 10.21 p.m. on the evening of Sunday 14 April 1912 that the *Californian* 'was forced to stop when she unexpectedly came up to a vast field of pack ice directly ahead of her'.[8] Here the ship remained until 5.15 a.m. next morning, Monday 15 April 1912.[9]

Halpern calculated that *Californian* was 17 nautical miles distant when *Titanic* sent out her SOS position, 'not the 19½ to 20 miles that was later claimed by Captain Lord'.[10]

When Captain Lord instructed Apprentice James Gibson to continued signalling the vessel that had fired the distress rockets by Morse lamp, why, said Halpern, had it 'never occurred to anyone after seeing these rockets, to wake up [*Californian*'s Marconi operator] Cyril Evans and try to contact the vessel by wireless'?[11]

It was not until after 5 a.m. on the morning of Monday 15 April 1912, when daylight had dawned, that Evans was finally awakened, and learned from Mount Temple's wireless operator John Durrant that *Titanic* had struck an iceberg and sunk.[12]

An unresolved issue

There is a wide discrepancy, both in various eyewitness accounts and in subsequent investigations as to just how near to *Titanic* the ship which was assumed to be SS *Californian* was at the crucial time. Lightoller said 'a couple of miles'; Gracie 'only four or five miles off'; Captain Lord '19½ to 20 miles'; Halpern '17 nautical miles distant'. This has given rise to speculation that there was another (unidentified) ship in the vicinity, but this has not been proven.

So much for the heap of criticism piled on to the shoulders of Captain Lord. But what did he himself have to say in his own defence?

30

Captain Lord's Defence

Stanley Lord, Master Mariner and Captain of the *Californian*, aged 35 and married to Mabel Henrietta (née Tutton) was born in Bolton, Lancashire on 13 September 1877. Lord was therefore 27 years Captain Smith's junior.

Lord was questioned at great length at both the UK and US Inquiries. Aged thirty-five, he had been a mariner for twenty years, most recently as master of the *Antillian* (5,600 tons displacement), *Louisianian* (3,600 tons), *William Cliff* (3,350 tons), and now the *Californian*.

The steamship *Californian* was a Leyland Line (under the control of the International Mercantile Marine Company) vessel of 6,500 tons displacement, with a maximum speed of 12½ to 13 knots. She had a crew of 55 and carried 48 passengers. She carried 4 lifeboats, which could carry 218 persons, well in excess of what was required. All her lifeboats were equipped with 'a compass, lamp, oil', and a 'sea anchor', said Lord, and all were 'provisioned all the time with water and biscuits'.[1]

Californian's voyage

When, on 5 April 1912 the *Californian* set sail from London for Boston, USA, little could anyone have guessed the forthcoming drama which she would be caught up in! On this occasion she carried no passengers.[2]

Californian's ice warning to the *Antillian*

On Sunday 14 April 1912 at 7.30 p.m., Captain Lord of the *Californian* sent a message to the *Antillian* giving the position of three large icebergs 5 miles to the south of his vessel. When *Californian*'s wireless operator sent the same message to *Titanic*, he was told that the message had already been received, having been intercepted by that vessel.

Ice warnings received by the *Californian*

On Saturday 13 April Captain Lord received an ice warning from Captain Barr of the *Coronian*: 'Westbound steamers report bergs, growlers, and field ice 42° north from 40° 51', April 12'.

At 6.30 p.m. on the evening of Sunday 14 April Captain Lord received an ice warning from the *Parisian*: '41° 55' [latitude] 49° 14' [longitude], passed three large icebergs'.

In view of the warning from the Parisien, at 8 p.m. Captain Lord doubled the lookout. 'I was treating it with every respect', he declared. 'We had one man at the crow's nest and a man at the forecastle head [at the bow of the ship], and I was on the bridge myself with an officer, which I would not have been under ordinary conditions.' Why? 'Because we have passed bergs during the afternoon, and we had had a report of bergs from east-bound steamers.' There was no haze that night, he said.[3]

The SS *Californian* encounters field ice

At 10.21 p.m., *Californian* encountered field ice – a phenomenon which Lord had not experienced before – and his ship was forced to stop. The ice stretched as far as he could see 'to the northward and southward'. Was the *Californian* 'hemmed in' by the ice? No, said Lord, 'we were just floating about'. Lord remained on the bridge until 10.30 p.m., when the watch was discontinued.[4]

Ice warning issued by the *Californian*

At 11.07 p.m., *Californian* sent a message to *Titanic*. 'We told them we were stopped and surrounded by ice', said Lord. In fact, said Lord, 'we were surrounded by a lot of loose ice, and we were about a quarter of a mile off the edge of the [ice] field'. (By the following morning, when day dawned, it became clear that the ice covered an area 'about 26 miles long and from 1 to 2 miles wide', said Lord.) Did Lord order a lookout to kept, even though the vessel had stopped? Yes, he said, one man on lookout in the crow's nest. This was in case 'some of those big fellows [icebergs] come crunching along and get into it [the ice field]'. From start to finish, Lord said, he had no idea of *Titanic*'s position, but he sent the warning even so.

Similarly, Lord also ordered *Californian*'s wireless operator Cyril F. Evans to message other ships in the area. This was 'a message of advice', he said, 'to warn them, so that they would know if they were in the vicinity [of ice] or pass the word on to other steamers'.[5]

The mystery steamer

At 11 p.m. on Sunday 14 April, said Lord, he saw the lights of a steamer about 'six or seven miles away', which he was sure could not have been the *Titanic*. This was because the steamer was 'something like ourselves' in size, i.e. 6,500 tons. There was no communication between this vessel and the *Californian*. Even when *Californian*'s third officer attempted to communicate with her at a distance of 'about five miles', there was no response. At 11.30 p.m. the mystery vessel stopped, presumably on account of the ice. At 12.50 a.m. on Monday 15 April, she steamed on and the last *Californian*'s Second Officer Herbert Stone saw of her was at 2 a.m. at a distance of 'I think 8 [miles]', said Lord.[6]

Had Lord any idea 'what steamer that was'? 'Not the faintest', he replied. 'At daylight we saw a yellow-funnel steamer on the southwest of us, beyond where this man [the mystery vessel] had left, about 8 miles away'.[7]

Captain Lord takes a nap

Captain Lord had gone on duty at 7 a.m. on Sunday 14 April and he 'was on deck practically the whole day', he said, having received reports 'from east-bound steamers of the presence of ice'.

At 12.15 a.m. on Monday 15 April Lord had retired to the chart room. At 12.40 a.m. he received a report from Second Officer Stone to say that the mystery steamer had not changed her position. At 1.15 a.m. Stone told Lord via the 'speaking tube' that the mystery ship had altered her bearings 'towards the S.W.'. Also, 'he said he saw a white rocket'. But Lord did not believe the rocket was sent up by the *Titanic*. It was sometime after 1.30 a.m., said Lord, that he fell asleep, and as far as he was aware, he remained asleep until 4.30 a.m.[8]

The mystery of the masthead lights

Prior to 12 midnight on 14/15 April, Captain Lord and Second Officer Stone saw a vessel with one masthead light, but Third Officer Charles V. Groves saw a vessel with two. So, was the vessel they were looking at *Titanic* (which had two), or was it the mystery vessel?

Where was *Titanic* in relation to *Californian*?
'From the position we stopped ... to the position at which *Titanic* is supposed to have hit the iceberg' said Lord, the distance was 19½ to 19¾ miles. At that distance, would it be possible to see distress signals or Morse flashes, he was asked? He replied that he 'did not think it would be possible to see them at that distance. If they were seen, they would be so low on the horizon they might be [mistaken for] shooting stars'.[9]

When did Captain Lord learn the total number of rockets that the mystery steamer had fired?
It was only at about 5 a.m. on the morning of Monday 15 April, said Lord, that he learned from George F. Stewart his chief officer that the mystery vessel 'had fired several rockets on his watch'.[10]

Captain Lord's amnesia
At about 2 a.m. on the morning of 15 April Second Officer Stone sent Gibson, the Apprentice, to deliver a message to Captain Lord, to tell him that rockets had been 'sent up' by another vessel. However, said Lord, he was 'very likely was half awake', and he had 'no recollection of this Apprentice saying anything to me at all that morning'. He only learned about the rockets at 7 a.m. said Lord, when Stone 'said if they had been distress rockets, he would most certainly have come down and called me himself but he was not a little bit worried about it at all'.

Did Captain Lord recall Stone 'reporting at twenty minutes to three to you that morning through the [speaking] tube', and telling him that the mystery steamer 'had disappeared bearing south-west half west'? 'I do not remember it. He has told me that since', said Lord.[11]

Why was the mystery vessel firing rockets?
When Lord was asked this question, he said he had asked Second Officer Stone, 'Is that a company's signal?' Such signal rockets were used by ships to signal to one another (not to indicate distress). Whereupon Stone 'said he did not know'. However, 'If it had been a distress signal the officer on watch would have told me', said Lord. 'We sometimes get these company's signals which resemble rockets; they do not shoot as high, and they do not explode.' Lord was prepared to admit that 'it might have been a distress signal', but

'at the distance we were away from that steamer', which was 'about four to five miles … if it had been a distress signal, we would have heard the report'.

Lord was adamant that the steamer that had fired the rockets was not *Titanic*. Why? 'Because a ship like the *Titanic* at sea … is an utter impossibility for anyone to mistake.'

As for the rockets fired by *Titanic*, 'I thought we ought to have seen her signals at 19 miles', he said, 'that was the only thing that was worrying me'.[12] (This is at variance with what Lord had said previously.)

How to distinguish between distress signals and company signals

Although distress signals were white and company signals 'usually have some colours in them', said Lord, 'some companies have white'. In other words, a white rocket flash did not necessarily indicate distress.

'We never took them to be distress rockets', said Lord. 'The second officer [Stone]'s explanation to me of these rockets was that they were not distress rockets. The second officer, the man in charge of the watch, said most emphatically they were not distress rockets'. That was why no reference to the rockets was made in the ship's log.[13]

Lord was asked again, could *Titanic*'s Morse or rocket distress signals have been seen from the *Californian*? 'We could not have seen her Morse code, that is an utter impossibility', said Lord. As for the rockets, 'I do not think so. Nineteen and a half miles is a long way. It would have been way down on the horizon. It might have been mistaken for a shooting star or anything at all'.[14]

Titanic's CQD signal: If only!

At 12.25 a.m. on Monday 15 April *Titanic* sent out her first CQD signal (commonly regarded as an acronym for 'Come Quick, Danger!') However, at 11 p.m. the previous evening, *Californian*'s Marconi operator had retired for the night. Had he been at his post when *Titanic*'s CQD call was broadcast, would her Marconi apparatus have picked up such a message? 'Most certainly', said Captain Lord. In which case, could Captain Lord have navigated to her with any degree of safety in the night-time? 'It would have been most dangerous', he said. Also, 'I do not think we would have got there before the *Carpathia* did [i.e. at 4 a.m.], [even] if we would have got there as soon'.[15]

Titanic's demise

How did Lord first hear about the sinking of *Titanic*? From the *Frankfurt*, he said, shortly after 5 a.m. on Monday 15 April. And at 6 a.m. *Californian* received a message from the Virginian to say: '*Titanic* struck berg; wants assistance; urgent; ship sinking; passengers in boats'. His position 41° 46', longitude 40° 16'.[16]

SS *Californian* to the rescue!

Captain Lord immediately set sail, 'pushing through field ice', which prevented him taking a direct course. So instead of steaming for 19 miles, the *Californian* was obliged to steam for 30 miles in order to avoid the 'dense ice field'. From the ship's log, Lord read as follows:

> 'Six o'clock, proceeded slow, pushing through the thick ice.
> 6.20, clear of thickest of ice, proceeded full speed, pushing the ice.
> 8.30, stopped close to steamship *Carpathia*'.

The ship's average speed for the two-and-one-half hour journey was between 13 and 13½ knots.

By the time the *Californian* arrived at the scene of the tragedy at 8.30 a.m., the last of the survivors were being taken 'out of the [life]boats' by the *Carpathia*. Whereupon *Californian* cruised 'full speed in circles … round the vicinity of the wreck' until 11.20 a.m. looking for survivors but with no result. Did Lord see any icebergs during this time? 'I was surrounded by icebergs', he replied, the largest towering 'about 100 to 150 feet' above the surface of the water, and '700 or 800 feet' in width.[17]

Californian's Marconi wireless operator Cyril Evans

Evans went off duty at 11 p.m. on Sunday 14 April. Why therefore, when *Californian*'s second officer informed Lord via the 'speaking tube' that he had seen 'a white rocket', did Lord not rouse his Marconi operator from sleep? The mystery steamer, said Lord, 'had been in sight, the one that fired the rocket, when we sent the last message to the *Titanic*, and I was certain that the steamer was not the *Titanic*, and the operator said he had not [managed to contact or received any signals from] any other steamers, so I drew my conclusion that she [the mystery steamer] had not got any wireless. If she had had a Marconi [installation] … of course we could have got into communication'.[18]

31

Captains Smith and Lord Compared

Age
Captain Smith was aged 62; Captain Lord was aged 35.

Experience
The Extra Master's Certificate required a knowledge of advanced navigation. Captain Smith had held his Extra Master's Certificate for 24 years; Captain Lord for 11 years.

Ships
At 52,000 tons, *Titanic* was therefore 8 times the displacement of the largest ship that Lord had captained.

Prestige
Captain Smith was known as the 'Millionaires Captain'.

Previous record
Captain Smith had presided over several groundings and collisions; as far as is known Captain Lord's record was exemplary.

The circumstances of *Titanic*'s final voyage
RMS *Titanic* was sailing from Southampton to New York. SS *Californian* was sailing from Liverpool, UK to Boston, Massachusetts.

Ice warnings received
Captain Smith received several warnings that there were ice fields and icebergs ahead of him, all of which he ignored; Captain Lord took the ice warnings he received seriously.

Ice warnings issued

Captain Smith failed to issue any warnings to other shipping, even after he had entered the ice field; Captain Lord warned the ships around him that he had encountered icebergs, and an ice field which had obliged him, for the safety of his ship, to stop.

Unfair criticisms of Captain Lord

Lord was criticised for not waking his wireless operator from sleep when rockets were seen from another vessel. This vessel however could not have been *Titanic*, which was 19 miles away. Furthermore, *Californian*'s Officer of the Watch Herbert Stone did not believe them to be distress rockets, and he therefore did not feel it necessary to summon Captain Lord to the bridge.

Having set sail, it took the *Californian* 2½ hours to reach the scene of the wreckage of *Titanic*. Had *Californian*'s wireless operator Cyril Evans been awake and received *Titanic*'s CQD first distress call, sent out at 12.25 a.m. on 15 April, it is by no means certain that Captain Lord would have set sail immediately, given that it was pitch dark, that he was surrounded by ice, and that there were icebergs in the vicinity. He might have considered it far less risky to wait for daylight to dawn. However, had he risked setting sail during the night, his journey would undoubtedly have taken longer than the 2½ hours that it subsequently took him during the daytime, for obvious reasons, so he would arrived on the scene say 3½ hours later, i.e. no earlier than 4 a.m. In that case he could certainly have participated in the rescue, the last survivors having been rescued from the lifeboats by the *Carpathia* at 9 a.m.

To judge by the results, despite all warnings sent to him by fellow captains, Captain Smith had sailed at speed into an ice field in pitch darkness, and he had persisted in this even though the sound of the ice crashing against the hull was audible throughout the vessel could have left him and everyone aboard that this was the case. The result was that *Titanic* finished up at a depth of 12,000 feet at the bottom of the Atlantic Ocean, with immense loss of life to her passengers and crew. Captain Lord, by comparison, was wise and prudent, and in consequence he preserved his vessel.

32

Second Officer Lightoller's Account in More Detail

As senior surviving officer, Lightoller, in his account, might have been expected to provide more explanation of the decisions taken which led to *Titanic* colliding with the iceberg. It was, however, not quite so straightforward.

In his book *Titanic and Other Ships*, Lightoller largely reiterated what he had previously told the UK and US Enquiries:

As day followed day, officers and men settled down into the collar, and duty linked up with duty until the watches went by without pause or hitch. We were not out to make a record passage; in fact, the White Star Line invariably run their ships at reduced speed for the first few voyages. It tells in the long run, for the engines of a ship are very little different from the engines of a good car, they must be run in. It has often been said that, had not the *Titanic* been trying to make a passage the catastrophe would never have occurred. Nothing of the kind. She was certainly making good speed that night of April 14th, but not her best – nothing compared with what she would have been capable, in say a couple of years' time'. This is true. No one had suggested that *Titanic* was attempting to break any records.

'The disaster was just due to a combination of circumstances that [had] never occurred before and can never occur again', Lightoller continued. 'That may sound like a sweeping statement, yet it is a fact.'[1] If Lightoller meant circumstances such was *Titanic* sailing full pelt into an iceberg in pitch darkness, or if he meant encountering such an iceberg in the ship's path at that location and at that time of year, then *wrong on both counts*!

'All during that fatal day the sea had been like glass – an unusual occurrence for that time of the year – not that that caused any great worry. Again, there had been an extremely mild winter in the Arctic, owing to which, ice from the ice cap and glaciers had broken away in phenomenal quantities, and official reports say that never be-fore or since has there been known to be

Second Officer Lightoller's Account in More Detail   119

such quantities of icebergs, growler, field ice and float ice, stretching down with the Labrador current. In my fifteen years' experience on the Atlantic I had certainly never seen anything like it ...' That is as may be. However, records indicate that in 1912 and adjacent years, icebergs were by no means uncommon at that location and at that time of year.

'These were just some contributory causes that combined and brought into existence, conditions of which the officers of the ship were to a great extent ignorant.'[2] It is true that Captain Smith was not the best communicator as far as his officers concerned. And yet, when the ice warnings were posted up in the officers' chart room, they must all have realised the jeopardy in which he was placing the ship, yet not one of them sought to question his authority.

On that fateful night, was there any discussion between himself, and 'Mr Boxhall or Mr Murdoch or Mr Lowe regarding the proximity of the *Titanic* to ice', Third Officer Pitman was asked? The answer was no. Was there any discussion with the captain about ice. Again, the answer was no.[3]

As regards the risk of encountering icebergs, said Third Officer Pitman, he and his fellow officers 'spoke of it amongst ourselves'. This was a reference to himself, Murdoch, and Lightoller. At what time was that? 'Sunday', Pitman replied. 'It might have been about 8 o'clock [p.m.]. I do not remember the time.' 'You did not talk it over with the captain?' 'Oh, no, sir.' What was the gist of the conversation? 'We were just remarking that we should be in the vicinity of ice in Mr Murdoch's watch', which began at 10 p.m.[4] Clearly, Captain Smith preferred to remain aloof from all discussion, a feature of his behaviour which chimes perfectly with his character, as will be seen.

'Wireless reports were coming in through the day from various ships, of ice being sighted in different positions', continued Lightoller. 'Nor was that anything unusual at this time of the year, and none of the reports indicated the extent of the ice seen. A report would read 'iceberg (or icebergs) sighted in such and such a latitude and longitude'. Later on in the day we did get reports of ice sighted in larger quantities, and also two reports of field ice, but they were in positions that did not affect us'. Not immediately, perhaps, but surely this should have indicated the extra caution and extra vigilance were required both on the part of the lookouts and the Marconi operators.

'The one vital report that came through, but which never reached the bridge, was received at 9.40 p.m. from the *Mesaba* stating 'Ice report in Latitude 42N to 41–25N. Long. 49 to Long 50–30 W.' Saw much heavy pack ice, and great number [of] large icebergs. Also, field ice. Weather good, clear. Phillips, the wireless operator [telegraphist] on watch who received the message was not to know the extreme urgency of the warning or that we were at the time actually entering the area given by the *Mesaba* and are [i.e. an area] literally packed with icebergs, field ice, and growlers. He was very busy working wireless messages to and from Cape Race, also with his accounts. The junior operator, [telegraphist, Harold] Bride, of course knew nothing about this vital warning, being off duty and turned in. Later, when standing with others on the upturned boat, Phillips explained when I said that I did not recollect any *Mesaba* report: 'I just put the message under a paper weight at my elbow, just until I squared up what I was doing before sending it to the Bridge'. *That delay proved fatal and was the main contributory cause to the loss of that magnificent ship and hundreds of lives.*' That *Mesaba*'s message did not reach *Titanic*'s bridge was, of course, extremely regrettable, but several other ice warnings had already been received.

'Had I as Officer of the Watch, or the Captain become aware of the peril lying so close ahead and not instantly slowed down or stopped, we should have been guilty of culpable and criminal negligence.'[5] 'Criminal negligence' is precisely how the entire *Titanic* fiasco may be described!

'For the last hour of my watch [6 p.m. to 10 p.m.] on that never to be forgotten night I had taken up a stationary position on the bridge, where I had an unobstructed view right ahead, and perhaps a couple of points on either bow. That did not signify that I was *expecting* to see ice, but that there was the *possibility* of seeing ice, as there always is when crossing The Banks; ice *may* be sighted. In point of fact, under normal conditions, we should have probed to be [i.e. we would normally have been] well south of the usual ice limit; only in this case the ice limit had moved very many miles south, due solely to the immense amount of ice released in the Arctic.'[6] But surely, as soon as the ice warnings had been received, *Titanic* should either have hove to – i.e. come to a stop – as soon as darkness approached, or immediately have altered course to the south.

'In ordinary circumstances the cold current carrying the icebergs south, strikes the warm current flowing to the north-east and under-runs in – that is to say the cold current goes under the warm current, on the same principle that warm water always rises. The effect of this is to melt the iceberg around the water line. It soon 'calves' or breaks up into smaller pieces, which again break up, continuing to float in the warm surface current for a short time, until completely melted. And so, the work of disintegration goes on in an ever-increasing ratio, thereby forming the 'ice limit'.'[7] This shows that Lightoller was clearly aware of the potential perils of the Labrador Current.

'It is often said you can tell when you are approaching ice by the drop in temperature. The answer to that is, open a refrigerator door when the outside temperature is down, and see how close you have get, before you detect a difference. No, you would have to be uncomfortably close to 'smell' ice that way.'[8] his is patently untrue. Both passengers and crew members alike noticed the sudden and dramatic drop in temperature prior to *Titanic* colliding with the iceberg, a drop which signified that the vessel had now left the comparatively warm Gulf Stream and entered the freezing cold domain of the iceberg-bearing Labrador Current.

'Ten p.m. came and with it the change of the officers' watches. On the bridge, after checking over such things as position, speed, and so forth, the officers coming on deck usually have a few minutes chat with their opposite number before officially taking over. The senior officer coming on watch, hunts up his man in the pitch darkness, and just yarns for a few minutes, whilst getting his eyesight after being in the light. When he can see all right, he lets the other chap know and officially 'takes over'.'[9]

'Murdoch and I were old shipmates and for a few minutes – as was our custom – we stood there looking ahead and yarning over times and incidents, past and present. We both remarked on the ship's steadiness, absence of vibration, and how comfortably she was slipping along. Then we passed on to more serious subjects, such as the chances of sighting ice, reports of ice that had been sighted, and the positions. We also commented on the lack of definition between the horizon and the sky – which would make an iceberg all the more difficult to see – particularly if it had a black side, and that [if it] should be, by bad luck, turned our way. The side of an iceberg that has calved or broken away from its parent glacier will usually be black, where the fresh ice is showing, and is consequently more difficult to see at night. After considerable exposure, this side turns white like the rest.'[10] All the more reason to slow down, post an extra lookout or two, or even have to, as other ships had done, one might reasonably have thought!

'We were then making an easy 22 knots. It was pitch dark and Dead Cold. Not a cloud in the sky, and the sea like glass. The very smoothness of the sea was, again, another unfortunate circumstance that went to complete the chain. If there had been either wind or swell, the outline of the berg would have been rendered visible, through the water breaking at the base'.[11] But how could this possibly be the case, given the pitch darkness?

Said Lightoller, after Murdoch took over the watch at 10 p.m., 'the temperature on deck felt somewhere around the zero of Canada, although actually, it wasn't much below freezing, and I quickly rolled into my blankets. There I lay, turning over my past sins and future punishments, waiting until I could thaw and get to sleep.'[12] Surely Lightoller must have realised the significance of the suddenness of the drop in temperature, which he himself had remarked upon?

When the collision occurred, said Lightoller, 'I was just about ready for the land of nod, when I felt a sudden vibrating jar run through the ship. The time we struck was 12:00 p.m., April 14th of tragic memory, and it was about ten minutes later that the fourth officer, Boxhall opened my door, and, seeing me awake, quietly said, 'We've hit an iceberg'. I replied, 'I know you've hit something'. He then said, 'The water is up to F deck in the Mail Room'.[13]

'The decks in the modern liner are lettered from the boat deck downwards A, B, C, D, E, and so on. The fact of the water having reached 'F' deck showed me she had been badly holed but, at the time, although I knew it was serious, I had not a thought that it was likely to prove fatal; that knowledge was to come much later.'[14]

'She struck the berg well forward of the foremast, and evidently there had been a slight shelf protruding below the water. This pierced her bow as she threw her whole weight on the ice, some actually falling on her fore deck.' In fact, it was more likely to be the area of the keel, rather than the bow, which sustained the damage.

'The impact flung her bow off, but only by the whip or spring of the ship. Again, she struck, this time a little further aft. Each blow stove in a plate, below the water line, as the ship had not the inherent strength to resist.'[15]

'Had it been, for instance, the old *Majestic* or even the *Oceanic* the chances are that either of them would have been strong enough to take the blow and be bodily thrown off without serious damage.'

However:

> 'Then ships grew in size, out of all proportion to their strength, till one would see a modern liner brought with all the skill and care possible, fall slowly, and ever so gently on a knuckle [hard protuberance], to bend and dent a plate like a piece of tin.'[16]

> 'That is exactly what happened to the *Titanic*. She just bump, bump, bumped along the berg, holing herself each time, till she was making water in no less than six compartments, though, unfortunately, we were not to know this until much later.'

> 'Actually, the *Titanic* was so constructed and divided into watertight compartments that she would float with any two compartments full of water, and the margin of safety made it fairly certain that she would still have floated with even three or four forward compartments full up. Although the water would have been above the forward watertight bulkheads, it would still have been kept out of the rest of the ship, despite the fact that the forward part of her would have completely submerged. The whole ship would have assumed a fairly acute and mighty uncomfortable angle, yet, even so, she would, in all probability have floated – at least for some considerable time, perhaps all day. Certainly, for sufficient time for everyone to be rescued; and, just possibly, until she could have been beached. But she could not remain afloat when she was holed in the forward stokehold as well. That made the Fifth Compartment counting from forward, that was smashed in by the iceberg, and this finally sealed her fate.' As it turned out', Lightoller concluded, *Titanic* 'was holed in no less than six compartments along the starboard side and *nothing* could have saved her'.[17]

This is most certainly true.

Lightoller now made the most preposterous remark about his captain, Edward Smith, who, he said:

> 'was one of the ablest skippers on the Atlantic, and accusations of recklessness, carelessness, not taking due precautions, or driving his ship at too high a speed were absolutely and utterly unfounded.'[18] The

real question was not *whether* Captain Smith was reckless – which he undoubtedly was – but *why?* This will be addressed shortly.

Lightoller's account is frankly implausible and disingenuous in parts, so how may this be explained? Clearly the White Star Line's powers-that-be, having lost their prized and most prestigious vessel, would now be anxious to avoid a series of expensive lawsuits, so one may imagine Lightoller being taken to one side and told in no uncertain terms that if he admitted anything which might render the company liable to prosecution, then do not expect to remain in our employ hereafter!

33
Weaknesses in *Titanic*'s Design and Construction

Rivets

In an article entitled 'NIST [National Institute of Standards and Technology] Reveals How Tiny Rivets Doomed a *Titanic* Vessel', US science writer Michael E. Newman explained how, in 1998, US NIST metallurgist Professor Tim Foecke 'performed metallurgical and mechanical analyses on steel and rivet samples recovered from the *Titanic* debris field at the bottom of the ocean. His examinations determined that the wrought iron in the rivets contained three times today's allowable amount of slag'.

Slag: stony waste matter separated from metals during the smelting or refining of ore.[1]

The result was, said Newman, that the slag 'made the rivets less ductile and more brittle than they should have been when exposed to very cold temperatures – like those typically found in the icy seawater of the North Atlantic'.

Ductile: able to be deformed without losing toughness; pliable.[2]

The conclusion was, therefore, 'that *Titanic*'s collision with the iceberg caused the rivet heads to break off, popped the fasteners from their holes, and allowed water to rush in between the separated hull plates'. Corroboration of this statement is provided by 'photographs of *Titanic*'s sister ship, the RMS *Olympic*', taken after she 'collided with another vessel in 1911', which 'clearly show dozens of vacant holes in the hull from which rivets [had] popped'.[3]

The keel
Such a keel as *Titanic* possessed, could probably have withstood a gentle grounding at low speed. However, a grounding at high speed would undoubtedly have caused the plates of both the inner and outer hull on either side of the keel to buckle and to become dislodged, allowing water to enter into the compartments above. But in the hands of such a capable sailor as Captain Smith, this could never have happened, but of course, it did!

The bows
Titanic's bows could probably have withstood a head-on collision at slow speed without compromising the buoyancy of the ship, whereas at high speed it is likely that one that at least one of her forward compartments would have been breached. However, it appears that the keel, rather than the bow, was where the damage occurred.

The bulkheads
Wilding stated that 'if No. 6 Boiler Room [Compartment 5] and the three holds forward of it [Compartments 4,3, and 2], and the forepeak [Compartment 1] are flooded', then *Titanic* would 'undoubtedly' be 'lost'.[4] In fact, the evidence is that all six forward compartments were flooded. The question arises, could higher bulkheads have saved *Titanic*?

On Day 20 of the UK Inquiry a piece of evidence was presented that made all previous discussion about the height of *Titanic*'s bulkheads irrelevant: 'What is the evidence', F. Laing, lawyer representing Harland & Wolff, was asked, 'as to the place from which the water came into No. 4 Boiler Room?' – i.e. into Compartment Number 7. 'All the evidence is that it came up from under the floor', Laing replied. I.e. it did not cascade over the top of the adjacent bulkhead. This was taken to imply that an 'external lesion' – i.e. penetration of the hull of the ship *adjacent to and beneath* No. 4 Boiler Room was the cause of the ingress of water.[5] The same was evidently true in respect of the ingress of water into the first six forward compartments – i.e. the water encroached from the region of the keel. The conclusion from Laing's evidence is that *not six but seven forward compartments of Titanic's hull were punctured*. In other words, the damage to *Titanic*'s keel was *even greater* than hitherto realised.

Once sea water had entered *Titanic*'s watertight compartments on the starboard side, could it then have flowed 'from the starboard to the port side of the ship', Wilding was asked? Yes, once it had risen above the level of 'E' [upper] deck, he replied.[6]

34

Verdict of the UK and US Inquiries

The US Senate Investigation
The US Investigation, chaired by Senator William Alden Smith, commenced on 19 April 1912 and concluded of 25 May 1912. The Report was issued on 28 May 1912.

As regards the lifeboats, the Senate Investigation concluded that 'there was no system adopted for loading the boats; there was great indecision as to the deck from which boats were to be loaded; there was wide diversity of opinion as to the number of crew necessary to man each boat; there was no direction whatever as to the number of passengers to be carried by each boat, and no uniformity in loading them. The failure to utilize all the lifeboats to their recognized capacity for safety unquestionably resulted in the needless sacrifice of several hundred lives which might otherwise have been saved. The vessel was provided with lifeboats … for 1,176 persons, while but 706 were saved'.[1]

The US Senate Committee stated that 'the ice positions so definitely reported to the *Titanic* just preceding the accident located ice on both sides of the track or lane which the *Titanic* was following, and in her immediate vicinity'. Now came an implied and scathing criticism of Captain Smith: 'No general discussion took place among the officers; no conference was called to consider these warnings; no heed was given to them. The speed was not relaxed, the lookout was not increased, and the only vigilance displayed by the officer of the watch was by instructions to the lookouts to keep 'a sharp lookout for ice'.[2]

Furthermore, even though, when *Titanic* collided with the iceberg and the serious nature of the damage was realised, 'no general alarm was sounded, no whistle blown, and no systematic warning was given to the passengers'.[3]

Finally, Bartlett was asked if he could 'explain how it was that after *Titanic* struck the iceberg, only a 'very few of the crew, the deck hands and officers went to the boats to which they were stationed?' The ordinary seamen and firemen 'went where the officers ordered them', said Bartlett. 'Would not one of the results of having regular boat musters be that in an emergency the men who had been trained in ordinary circumstances to go to their proper boats would do so?' Bartlett agreed. 'They would go in their proper [i.e. designated] boats', he agreed.[4] Once again, because the thinking was that *Titanic* was unsinkable, a culture of complacency existed with the result that when disaster struck, the response was found wanting.

By contrast, the Senate Investigation Report was full of praise for Captain Arthur Henry Rostron of the *Carpathia*, who, after *Titanic*'s collision, 'doubled his lookout and exerted extra vigilance, putting an extra lookout on duty forward and having another officer on the bridge. The committee deems the course followed by Captain Rostron ... as deserving of the highest praise and worthy of especial recognition'.[5]

The UK Board of Trade Inquiry

The UK Inquiry commenced on 2 May 1912 at the Scottish Drill Hall, Buckingham Gate, London. It was presided over by judge Sir John Charles Bingham, Lord Mersey. The Inquiry heard from 94 witnesses who gave some 26,000 answers covering 26 specific aspects of the disaster. The hearing lasted until 3 July 1912 and the results were published on 30 July 1912.

The UK Inquiry addressed the question as to how many of *Titanic*'s watertight compartments had been breached as a result of her collision with the iceberg. The conclusion was that seawater had entered the first 6 compartments (the forepeak being counted as the first).[6]

'The Court, having carefully inquired into the circumstances of the above-mentioned shipping casualty, finds ... that the loss of the said ship was due to collision with an iceberg, brought about by the excessive speed at which the ship was being navigated.'

Under the heading 'Action That Should Have Been Taken', the UK Inquiry concluded that two courses of action were open to *Titanic*'s master, Captain Smith: 'The one was to stand [steer] well to the southward instead of turning up to a westerly course; the other was to reduce speed materially as night approached. He did neither'. Furthermore, 'the alteration of the course at 5.50 p.m. was so insignificant that it cannot be attributed to any intention to avoid ice. This deviation brought the vessel back to within about two miles of the customary route before 11.30 p.m. And there was certainly no reduction of speed'.

The question therefore arose, 'why, then, did the Master persevere in his course and maintain his speed?' The Inquiry concluded that this was a practice that 'had been justified by experience, no casualties having resulted from it'. In that case why had ships in the vicinity taken the trouble to warn Captain Smith of the possible danger, and why had Captain Rostron of the *Carpathia* and Captain Lord of the *Californian* actually stopped, rather than take the risk of venturing into the ice fields?

'In these circumstances I am not able to blame Captain Smith. He made a mistake, a very grievous mistake, but one in which, in face of the practice and of past experience, negligence cannot he said to have had any part; and in the absence of negligence it is, in my opinion, impossible to fix Captain Smith with blame'.[7] In other words, Captain Smith was fully justified in ignoring warnings from other vessels, and failing to take the kind of precautions which their captains had taken!

35

J. Bruce Ismay's Testimony to the UK and US Inquiries

British Wreck Commissioner's Inquiry
Joseph Bruce Ismay, member of the firm Ismay, Imrie & Co. (registered in Liverpool) and Managing Director of the Ocean Steam Navigation Company was aged 49 years at the time of the *Titanic* disaster.

Ismay had chosen to travel to New York aboard *Titanic* not as a mere first class passenger on her maiden voyage, but because in his capacity as managing director or as President of the American Trust he was 'interested in the ship' and desired 'to see how the vessel behaved'. The White Star Company was 'building another new ship, and we naturally wanted to see how we could improve on our existing ships'.[1] In fact, eight more vessels were built by Harland & Wolff in the year 1912.

Was *Titanic* unsinkable?
Was it Ismay's view, and also the view of his company, 'that the *Titanic* was unsinkable'? 'We thought she was', he replied. On what grounds? 'Because we thought she would float with two of the largest compartments full of water, and that the only way that those compartments were at all likely to be damaged was in case of collision – another ship running into her and hitting her on the bulkhead.'[2]

***Titanic*'s design features**
What instructions had been given to Harland & Wolff in regard to *Titanic*'s safety, Ismay was asked? 'We were very anxious indeed to have a ship which would float with her two largest watertight compartments full of water', Ismay replied. This was in the event of another ship hitting her 'broadside on'. The same applied to the *Olympic*.[3]

Shipping lanes (or 'Tracks')
Ismay was asked whether he was familiar with the fact that 'different tracks' (designated shipping lanes) were 'marked upon the charts. Different tracks for different seasons of the year?' 'Yes', he replied. And that this was 'for the purpose of avoiding ice'? 'Not entirely', he replied. And this was the reason why 'a more southerly track' was adopted 'during a certain period of the year?' 'That is true.' Ismay was asked, had he 'no curiosity to ascertain whether or not you would be travelling in the region in which ice was reported?' 'I had not', he replied. This, of course is scarcely credible!

Shipping regulations in respect of ice
Ismay confirmed that instructions as to navigation were contained in a volume entitled *Ships' Rules*, a copy of which was given to every officer on his appointment to the ship, and finally in a framed notice which was displayed in the chart room. But was there 'nothing specifically directed to the question of ice in any of these regulations?' he was asked. That was correct, Ismay replied. Was that 'left to the discretion of the Commander?' 'Certainly' he said.[4] Ismay was asked specifically, were any instructions given to White Star Line captains travelling from the United Kingdom to New York 'with reference to ice'. 'Not that I know of', he replied.

Ismay was appraised of the fact that by contrast, the Canadian Pacific Railway fleet was issued with instructions to the effect that their captains were 'not to enter an ice field … under any conditions … no matter how light it may appear'.[5]

It appears, however, that although *Titanic* was on the very edge of an ice field when the collision occurred, the vessel had not actually entered it.

Exchange of information in respect of ice
With regard to the whereabouts of ice, was there an interchange of information between the shipping companies before the start of any voyage, Ismay was asked, was all the information that had been received by *Titanic* in this way, up to date? Yes, he replied, every notice of ice received by any company was forwarded to the other companies, and there was a 'system of interchange of information between the captains'.[6]

The ice warning from the *Baltic*, and what became of it

Ismay was asked whether, on Sunday 14 April 1912, he had received information from *Titanic*'s captain, Edward Smith, of ice in the vicinity. 'The captain handed me a Marconi message which he had received from the *Baltic* on the Sunday', Ismay replied. This was 'just before lunch'. The message, which was addressed to Captain Smith, *Titanic*, was sent at 11.52 a.m. and read as follows. This was the aforementioned warning of icebergs and field ice at 'latitude 41.51 N., longitude 49.52 W'. Said Attorney General Sir Rufus Isaacs (representing the Board of Trade), 'we attribute very great importance to that particular message; we think it is of very great importance'.

Ismay was now asked if the message from the RMS *Baltic* was handed to him by Captain Smith because he was the managing director of the company? 'I do not know; it was a matter of information', he replied.[7]

In respect of *Titanic* receiving the telegram from RMS *Baltic*, was Ismay aware of what was the normal practice regarding telegrams in cases such as this? 'I believe the practice was to put them up in the chart room for the officers', he replied. 'Was not the Marconigram from the *Baltic* essentially a message affecting navigation?' In other words, could receipt of such a telegram lead to an alteration of the ship's course? 'Yes', Ismay replied. 'Then will you say why, under those circumstances, with that knowledge, you put that Marconigram into your pocket?', where it had remained 'for something like five hours … until it was asked for by Captain Smith late in the evening?' 'Ten minutes past seven, I think it was, he asked me for it', said Ismay. 'And you suggest that you put it in your pocket simply in a fit of absent-mindedness?' 'Yes, entirely', Ismay replied.

Ismay admitted that he 'knew we were approaching the region of ice, yes'. This was because of the Marconi message sent from RMS *Baltic*. And 'that you would be in the region of ice some time on that Sunday night?' 'I believe so, yes.' How did he know? 'I think the information I got was from Dr O'Loughlin, who said we had turned the corner.' This was Francis W. N. O'Loughlin, the ship's surgeon, who 'had been in the service over 40 years'.

Ismay confessed that he knew 'turning the corner' meant altering course 'more to the northward'. Did he know 'that that would bring you nearer to the region of ice which had been reported to you?' he was asked. 'The Marconi message did not convey any meaning to me as to the exact position of that ice', Ismay replied, and furthermore, 'I do not understand latitude and longitude'.

This latter statement, by a person of such high rank in the world of shipping, is frankly implausible; after all, globes (spherical representations of the earth) were to be found in those times in shipping offices, private houses, even in children's playrooms! The truth is that Ismay was distancing himself from taking any responsibility for or even commenting on the ice warnings or for Captain Smith's decision-making process.

Having 'turned the corner' and followed the track to New York, 'you may meet ice, either field ice, I suppose – infrequently apparently – or icebergs?' Ismay was asked. 'Certainly icebergs', he replied, 'but I should hardly think it was possible for field ice to be there'.[8] In fact, although there was evidently no field ice in the vicinity when *Titanic* struck the iceberg, photographs of the scene of the disaster taken the following morning show field ice as far as the eye could see.

But surely, Ismay was asked, 'it was possible to ascertain whether the latitude and longitude designated in that Marconigram would be a track that you would have to cross?' But he continued in the same vein. 'No. That is for the captain of the ship. He was responsible for the navigation of the ship. I had nothing to do with the navigation.' Technically, this was true, but surely, given his position as Managing Director of the Ocean Steam Navigation Company, and given the fact that Captain Smith had drawn the Marconigram to his attention, some reaction from him might have been expected, especially as the safety of the ship was at stake?[9] Instead, he simply put the Marconigram in his pocket and forgot about it!

Had Ismay received reports of his ships 'meeting icebergs on the voyage to the United States' previously? 'Oh yes', he replied.[10] Ismay was asked to confirm that the Marconigram handed to him by Captain Smith indicated that there were 'quantities of field ice in the track' along which *Titanic* was travelling, and that from the information received by this wireless telegram the ship 'would certainly within less than 24 hours be encountering field ice' if it 'pursued the same course'. 'I believe that is so', he said. Did it strike Ismay 'as a serious thing' that field ice would shortly be encountered? 'No, I do not think it did', he replied.[11]

This statement by Ismay is illogical in that sections of field ice would be expected to melt before the icebergs, which were larger. Therefore, if field ice was present, it is more than likely that icebergs would be present also.

J. Bruce Ismay's Testimony to the UK and US Inquiries   135

If Captain Smith 'thought he would meet field ice along that track would you expect him to take steps to avoid meeting it?' 'Certainly', replied Ismay. 'And to keep off that track along which he would meet it?' 'If he thought it necessary to do so'. Did Ismay 'say nothing to the Captain at all about it?' 'I did not.' 'Not ask him whether he was going to change his course?' 'No.' 'Nor he to you?' 'No.'

Ismay was therefore in doubt as to what Captain Smith's duties and responsibilities were, and he regarded this as being solely in the captain's domain.

Ismay's comment on lookouts
Should the White Star Company have issued instructions for extra precautions to be taken, such as employing extra lookouts, when a ship was in the vicinity of ice, Ismay was asked? No, he replied, this was solely the responsibility of the captain. 'Do not you think, as ice was reported in your track, and as you expected to be in the presence of ice, that the look-out should have been doubled?' 'I do not', replied Ismay.[12] It was pointed out to Ismay that the Canadian Pacific Railway fleet was issued with instructions to the effect that if ice was expected, the lookout was always doubled. 'You do not issue any similar instructions to your captain's?', he was asked. The answer was 'No'.[13] The impression gained is that Ismay had washed his hands of any responsibility whatsoever and was content to let others carry the proverbial can.

Ismay's comments of the speed of the ship
Was it Ismay's view, that his 'captains and officers' were 'discharging their duty in crossing the Atlantic, when ice is reported to them, in going ahead at full speed and taking no extra precautions?' 'So long as they can see the object far enough ahead to be able to avoid it', he replied. This is a reasonable statement to make, on the face of it. However, on the night in question, the visibility was *virtually zero!*[14]

United States Senate Inquiry
On Day 1 of the US Senate Inquiry, Ismay stated as follows: 'In the first place, I would like to express my sincere grief at this deplorable catastrophe'.[15]

Did 'the designers and builders' of ships 'intended for the North Atlantic' where ice and icebergs may be encountered build them with any 'special reference' to their 'resistance at the bow', he was asked? In other words, were such ships constructed with specially strengthened bows? 'No, sir', replied Ismay.[16]

Ismay was asked if Captain Smith was in good health, during *Titanic*'s final voyage from Southampton. 'As far as I saw ... as far as I was able to judge, at least', he replied.[17]

Was *Titanic* on the right track? Yes, replied Ismay, the ship was 'on the extreme southern route for the west-bound ships', though he did not know *Titanic*'s longitude and latitude.[18]

In respect of the 'telegram' (Marconigram) from RMS *Baltic*, said Ismay, it was 'very difficult to place the time' when Captain Smith had handed it to him. 'I do not know whether it was in the afternoon or immediately before lunch; I am not certain', he said. 'I did not pay any particular attention to the Marconi message – it was sent from the *Baltic* – which gave the position of some ice. I handed it back to Capt. Smith, I should think about 10 minutes past 7 on Sunday evening.' According to Ismay, Captain Smith told him, 'I want it to put up in the officers' chart room'. That is the only conversation I had with Capt. Smith in regard to the telegram. When he handed it to me, he made no remark at all.'[19]

What possible reason could Captain Smith have for entrusting Ismay with so vital an ice warning, thus ensuring a delay of 7 hours or so before it was posted up in the officers' chart room in the normal way? There are several possible reasons:

That he wished to conceal the warning from his officers for as long as possible, in case they had the temerity to question him about why he was sailing *Titanic* directly into the path of an ice field?; that he thought it his duty to warn Ismay of the impending danger, even though he himself chose to ignore that danger?; that he arrogantly believe that rules, regulations, protocols, and safety measures did not apply to him?

Ismay was asked whether he agreed that if *Titanic* was 'approaching ice in the night it would be desirable, would it not, to slow down?' To this he replied, 'I say no. I am not a navigator'. This prompted a swift retort from the Attorney-General, who was clearly beginning to lose patience: 'You are not quite frank with us, Mr Ismay'. 'I should say if a man can see far enough to clear ice, he is perfectly justified in going full speed', Ismay continued. Was it Ismay's view, 'that the faster you could get out of the region [of ice] the better'? 'Assuming the weather was perfectly fine, I should say the captain was perfectly justified in going full speed', Ismay replied, and 'so far as I could judge', he said, 'it was a perfectly fine, clear night'. But 'what is the object of continuing at full speed through the night if you expect to meet ice?', Ismay was asked. 'I presume that the man [Captain Smith, presumably] would be anxious to get through the ice region. He would not want to slow down upon the chance of a fog coming on', was Ismay's reply.

However, contrary to the statements of others, said Ismay, *Titanic* had 'never had been at full speed' during her transatlantic voyage. 'The full speed of the ship is 78 revolutions', he said. 'She works up to 80. So far as I am aware, she never exceeded 75 revolutions. She had not all her boilers on [i.e. in operation]. None of the single-ended boilers were on'. However, 'It was our intention, if we had fine weather on Monday afternoon or Tuesday [15th or 16th April], to drive the ship at full speed. That, owing to the unfortunate catastrophe, never eventuated.'[20]

Again, Ismay's argument in respect of the advisability of travelling into a known ice field at a speed in excess of 20 knots is flawed on two counts. Firstly, although it was a clear night, it was pitch dark. Secondly, whether or not there was fog, the visibility would still have been zero![21] Ismay stated that at daybreak on the Monday morning, 'I should think I saw four or five icebergs'.[22] QED!

There was an occasion, however, when Ismay's mask slipped. In her affidavit, Mahala Douglas quoted Mrs Emily Ryerson, whose 'story was told in the presence of Mrs Meyer, of New York, and others'. This was Leila (née Saks), wife of Edgar J. Meyer of Manhattan who was travelling with her. Said Mrs Ryerson, 'Sunday afternoon Mr. Ismay, whom I know very slightly, passed me on the deck. He showed me, in his brusque manner, a Marconigram, saying, 'We have just had news that we are in the icebergs'.' 'Of course, you will slow down', I said. 'Oh, no', he replied, 'we will put on more boilers and get out of it'.[23] Ismay thus revealed that he *totally concurred* with Captain Smith and approved of his *reckless and foolhardy behaviour*!

For all Ismay's obfuscations and clearly implausible protestations of ignorance, he did attempt to make some sort of amends. As regards the remaining ships of the White Star line, he said, as soon as the rescue vessel *Carpathia* had landed the survivors, instructions had been given 'that no ship belonging to the I.M.M. Co. [International Mercantile Marine

Company] is to leave any port unless she has sufficient boats on board for the accommodation of all the passengers and the whole of the crew'.[24] He also declared that after 'this horrible accident … the whole question of life-saving appliances' on ships would be 'very carefully' reviewed. Had he himself 'taken any steps in that direction since the accident'? No, he replied, but as soon as he returned home, he promised to take up the matter 'with our shipbuilding friends and with our experts'.[25]

What if Titanic had not made that fatal turn to port?

Ismay was asked his opinion, as to the likely outcome should *Titanic* have met the iceberg head-on. 'I think the ship would have crushed her bows in, and might not have sunk', he said. However, 'I think it would have taken a very brave man to have kept his ship going straight on [into] an iceberg. I think he should have endeavoured to avoid it'.[26]

Ismay's opinion as to the damage sustained

Ismay was asked if he knew 'how far the double bottom of the *Titanic* extended'? 'I should think the whole of the bottom, sir; the whole width of the ship', he replied. Therefore 'contact with the iceberg must have been above the double bottom, must it not? My impression is that the bilge of the ship was ripped out by the iceberg; simply torn right along. I think it ripped the ship up, right along the side'.[27]

Although Ismay was aware 'That we would be in the ice region on Sunday night', he said, he had not consulted the captain or any of the officers in regard to the matter. 'It was absolutely out of my province', he said. 'I am not a navigator. I was simply a passenger on board the ship.'[28] Clearly Ismay was anxious, at all costs, to distance himself from the tragedy of *Titanic*.

All the passengers that he saw were wearing 'life preservers', Ismay declared.[29] Finally, he stated that he had been 'in bed myself, asleep when the accident happened' – if 'accident' it can be called!

Morgan Robertson's Prophetic Novella: The Wreck of the Titan Or, *Futility* (1898): What If?

In 1898, 14 years prior to the *Titanic* disaster, a novella entitled *The Wreck of the Titan or, Futility* by Morgan Robertson was published. Morgan Andrew Robertson, born in 1861, was a US author of short stories and novels. He had gone to sea as a cabin boy and served in the merchant service from 1868 to 1899, rising to the position of first mate.

The similarity of the story to the *Titanic* disaster, beginning with the very name, '*Titan*', and featuring the eponymous fictional British ocean liner that sailed on the North Atlantic route is uncanny!

Titan, at 75,000 tons, 'is described as 'the largest craft afloat, and the greatest of the works of men' – as was the real-life *Titanic*, at 52,310 tons. 'Two brass bands, two orchestras and a theatrical company' entertained the passengers 'during waking hours'. *Titanic* had one orchestra, with 8 musicians.

From *Titan*'s 'lofty bridge, ran hidden telegraph lines [cables] to the bows, stern, engine room, crow's nest on the foremast, and to all parts of the ship where work was done, each wire terminating in a marked dial with a movable indicator, containing in its scope every order and answer required in handling the massive hulk, either at the dock or at sea – which eliminated, to a great extent, the hoarse, nerve-racking shouts of officers and sailors'. *Titanic* was similarly equipped with her own telegraph and telephone systems.

'From the bridge, engine room, and a dozen places on her deck, the ninety-two doors of nineteen water-tight compartments could be closed in half a minute by turning a lever. These doors would also close automatically in the presence of water.' *Titanic*'s vertical bulkheads divided the ship into 16 compartments.

'With nine compartments flooded the ship would still float, and as no known accident of the sea could possibly fill this many ....' It was reckoned that *Titanic* could remain afloat even if two of her compartments were flooded. Finally, 'the steamship *Titan* was considered practically unsinkable'. This was certainly the view of Captain Smith, in respect of *Titanic*!

Titan, like *Titanic*, was 'built of steel throughout, and for passenger traffic only', although the latter was also a mail ship. 'In short, she was a floating city – containing within her steel walls all that tends to minimize the dangers and discomforts of the Atlantic voyage – all that makes life enjoyable.' *Titanic*'s first class passengers would certainly have concurred with this latter sentiment!

'Unsinkable – indestructible, she carried as few [life] boats as would satisfy the laws.' *Titanic* in fact carried more lifeboats than were stipulated by the Board of Trade. 'These, twenty-four in number, were securely covered and lashed down to their chocks on the upper deck, and if launched would hold five hundred people.' However, as there were 'three thousand berths in the passengers', officers', and crew's quarters, this was sufficient to accommodate only one person in every six who sailed aboard the *Titan*. *Titanic*, similarly, was woefully short of lifeboat accommodation, having capacity for only 1,178 people.

Titan 'carried no useless, cumbersome life-rafts; but – because the law required it', sufficient cork lifejackets were provided', as with *Titanic*, 'while about twenty circular lifebuoys were strewn along the rails'. *Titanic* had 48 lifebuoys ('rings').

'In view of her absolute superiority to other craft,[3] a rule of navigation thoroughly believed in by some captains, but not yet openly followed, was announced by the steamship company to apply to the *Titan*: She would steam at full speed in fog, storm, and sunshine, and on the Northern Lane Route, winter and summer, for the following good and substantial reasons: First, that if another craft should strike her, the force of the impact would be distributed over a larger area if the *Titan* had full headway, and the brunt of the damage would be borne by the other. Second, that if the *Titan* was the aggressor she would certainly destroy the other craft, even at half-speed, and perhaps damage her own bows; while at full speed, she would cut her in two with no more damage to herself than a paintbrush could remedy. In either case, as the lesser of two evils, it was best that the smaller hull should suffer. A third reason was that, at full speed, she could be more easily steered out of danger, and a fourth, that in case of an end-on collision with an iceberg – the only thing afloat that she could not conquer – her bows would be crushed in but a few feet further at full than at half speed, and at the most three compartments would be flooded – which would not matter with six more to spare.'

Although the steamship company which owned *Titan* may have promoted such a reckless policy, this was certainly not the policy of the White Star Line, which preferred to leave such decisions to the individual ship's captains concerned. However, judging by his behaviour, such a reckless policy does seem to be more in keeping with the views of *Titanic*'s Captain Smith.

'When the watch turned out at midnight, they found a vicious half-gale blowing from the northeast, A fog-bank, into which the ship had plunged in the afternoon, still enveloped her – damp and impenetrable; and into the grey, ever-receding wall ahead, with two deck officers and three lookouts straining sight and hearing to the utmost, the great racer was charging with undiminished speed. In the case of *Titanic*, it was not fog that her officers and lookouts had to contend with at midnight on Sunday 14 April 1912, but fog, into which she too charged with 'undiminished speed'. Similarly, the officer's instructions to lookout Rowland in the crow's nest to 'Keep your eyes open – keep a sharp lookout', was uncannily similar to the instructions issued from the bridge by Sixth Officer Moody to *Titanic*'s lookouts, which were to keep 'a sharp lookout for ice'.

Not surprisingly, given the instructions issued by *Titan*'s steamship company, disaster ensued when the ship collided with another vessel and cut that vessel clean in two, despite *Titan*'s helmsman's attempts to avoid it.

Titan's Captain Bryce, who hoped to cover the whole matter up, said to Roland, 'You are aware, of course, that nothing could be done [i.e. have been done], either to avert this terrible calamity, or to save life afterward'. But Roland would not be silenced. 'Nothing at a speed of twenty-five knots an hour in a thick fog, sir', the lookout replied. Worse was to follow.

Lieutenant Matthew F. Maury (1806–1873) was a US oceanographer and naval officer whose book *Wind and Current Charts: Gales in the Atlantic*, showing sailors how to use the ocean's currents and winds to best advantage, was published in 1857. When the first officer asked Rowland what his opinion was on 'Maury's 'idea ... of locating the position of ice in a fog by the rate of decrease in temperature as approached', he replied, 'Not to any definite result. But it seems to be only a matter of calculation, and time to calculate. Cold is negative heat, and can be treated like radiant energy, decreasing as the square of the distance'. In other words, a sudden sharp drop in temperature was a reliable indication of the presence of ice, a fact which Second Officer Lightoller, for one, failed to acknowledge. 'The officer stood a moment, looking ahead and humming a tune to himself; then, saying: 'Yes, that's so', returned to his place.'

Suddenly, "Ice", yelled the lookout; 'ice ahead. Iceberg. Right under the bows'. As with *Titanic*, the iceberg was only spotted at the very last minute. The iceberg which confronted *Titan* was 'a hundred feet high'; that which confronted *Titanic* was an estimated 50 to 100 feet high. Now came a 'deafening noise of steel, scraping and crashing over ice'.

Had *Titan*'s bows impacted with the 'perpendicular wall' of the iceberg, 'the elastic resistance of bending plates and frames would have overcome the momentum with no more damage to the passengers than a severe shaking up, and to the ship than the crushing in of her bows and the killing, to a man, of the watch below. She would have backed off, and, slightly down by the head', and 'finished the voyage at reduced speed'. However, as with *Titanic*, *Titan* had beached on the iceberg's ledge, 'at the rate of fifty feet a second', compared with *Titanic*'s 22 knots, thus 'puncturing the sides of the ship, whereas with *Titanic* it was the area of the keel that was punctured, and flooding the engine rooms and boiler rooms so that she sank.

Roland's adventure continued as he rescued a little girl, Myra; set foot on the iceberg; and fought with and killed a polar bear that was menacing them![1]

Had *Titanic*'s Captain Smith, or his partner in crime J. Bruce Ismay read Morgan Robertson's book prior to setting sail on her maiden voyage, would they have behaved any differently? The answer is no, for both were convinced both of their absolute infallibility, and of the ship's invincibility.

37

Eva Hart: A Survivor's Account

Aboard *Titanic* was Benjamin Hart, a builder, who was emigrating to Canada aboard *Titanic* with his wife Esther and their daughter Eva, aged 7 years as second class passengers. Only Eva and her mother survived the sinking.

When Eva was interviewed in 1992, she said of Captain Smith, who her family met with on several occasions aboard ship, 'He was very nice to me'. Eva was highly articulate, and her memory was outstandingly good.

Before setting sail, said Eva, her mother 'had this dreadful premonition', that 'something dreadful will happen!'. She said to her husband, 'Now, I don't want any more unhappiness about this, but my mind is made up. I will not go to bed in this ship. I shall sleep in the daytime, and I will sit up at night'. To this, Benjamin replied, 'If you're going to be stupid, I can't stop you!' 'I know, but I'm going to do it', Esther insisted, 'and she did', said Eva. 'And she sat up Wednesday night, Thursday night, Friday night, and on Saturday night [13 April 1912] she heard an odd sound, and she awakened my father and made him go up on the deck. And he came back, and he told her that it was ice flows that she could hear grinding against the side of the ship, and not to be so silly. And at breakfast the next morning other people said they had gone up on deck and they had heard this kind of noise, and they agreed it was ice flows.' This confirms that *Titanic* was not on the perimeter of the ice field; the vessel had sailed *right into it*.

'My mother said, 'Well surely, if there is ice abundant in the sea, there could be icebergs'. And this officer at our table, he said, 'Nonsense, an iceberg is an enormous thing! We should see an iceberg! There's nothing to be afraid of'.'

On Sunday night [14 April 1912], said Eva, 'Everyone was gambling', but 'my father would have nothing to do with it and he went to bed quite early. Mother sat down to sew, and father went to sleep. At ten minutes to twelve', said Eva, her mother 'felt a slight bump. It was just like a train pulling into the station. It just jerked it was very slight, but she said she knew that it was this dreadful something, and she awakened my father and me and my father said no, he wasn't going up on deck again after the night before. But she literally pulled him out of bed and made him go up. And she then said she was going to dress me, but I was sleepy and very naughty, and I said 'I'm not going to be dressed. I'm going back to bed".

Benjamin returned, wrapped Eva in a blanket, 'put his very thick coat' on Esther 'and put another on himself'. They then took the lift up onto the boat deck. 'If we hadn't done that at that time', said Eva, 'I doubt very much if I would be talking to you today'.

The lifeboats 'weren't launched very quickly', said Eva, 'because at first, no one thought anything was going to happen. My father spoke to an officer, and he said, 'We are going to launch the lifeboats, but you'll all be back in time for breakfast. My father put me in a lifeboat and told me to be good. He said to me, 'hold Mummy's hand', and I thought he was coming in after me, but he didn't. Then it dawned on me, of course, that he wasn't coming. I didn't see him anymore.'

'The collision was at ten minutes to twelve, and *Titanic* sank at twenty minutes past two. So, if we had had enough lifeboats, no one would have died that night at all.'

Eva said that she clearly saw *Titanic* break in half. She also saw another ship that was in the vicinity clearly, but she could not state categorically that it was the SS *Californian*. 'I saw our rockets being fired, which that ship must have seen.' But she could not understand why there was no response. 'In the middle of the Atlantic Ocean' and 'in the middle of the night, rockets must mean trouble', she said.

Before *Titanic* sank, said Eva, 'the band played a version of the hymn 'Nearer my God to Thee'. 'We were down in the water [i.e. in the lifeboat] by then', she said.

Previously there had been no panic, but 'when the others started coming up from the cabins' and saw that 'there were no lifeboats, there *was* panic', said Eva. 'We could hear it, definitely. But the most dreadful sound of all was the sound of people drowning; the screams; absolutely ghastly! In the silence that followed, it was as if the whole world stood still that night. Once the light had gone, the ship had gone, the sound of it had gone, it was dreadful.'

It was impossible for small children to climb the ladder that was lowered down to the lifeboats from the *Carpathia*, so they were put into a sack, a small number at a time, and this was placed in a net and hauled up on deck; yet another terrifying experience for Eva!

Once aboard the *Carpathia*, said Eva, 'one of the most pathetic things must have been' when 'the whole of the next day, these poor women such as my mother roamed about the ship, looking to see if they could see the husbands that they had left behind. But they never found anyone there.'

Finally, said Eva, on arrival at New York, her mother decided that she was not going to emigrate to Canada, and she and Eva returned to the UK.[1]

38

Bernice Palmer, Her Camera, and the Iceberg

Bernice Gardner Palmer was born on 10 January 1893 at Waterloo, Ontario, Canada. Her father Frederick Douglas Palmer was a US bookkeeper, married to Florence Cleugh (née Brydon) of Scottish descent. She had an elder brother, Douglas.

On date April 1912 19-year-old Bernice and her mother Florence set sail from New York on the *Carpathia*, bound for a Mediterranean cruise. On the morning of Monday 15 April 1912 commotion roused her from sleep. Said she:

'A few minutes after that, the constant rhythm of the engines stopped and the boat was very still, so I knew something was wrong. And I looked out of the porthole and saw several small [life] boats with people in them rowing towards the ship.'[1] *Carpathia* was rescuing survivors from the sunken *Titanic*.

It so happened that prior to the voyage, Bernice had received a Kodak Brownie box camera, No. 2A, Model B, and she now used it to record the dramatic events that were taking place before her eyes. She photographed the approaching lifeboats; the survivors huddled together on the deck of the *Carpathia*, many in their nightclothes, or evening dress, having had no time to prepare, or clothing generously donated by *Carpathia*'s passengers.

When *Carpathia* returned to New York, Bernice was approached by a reporter from photographic company Underwood & Underwood, who offered her ten dollars for permission to develop the photographs and return them to her. He also got her to sign a contract, relinquishing the reproduction rights to his company.

What is fascinating is that one of the photographs taken by Bernice is of a large iceberg which is generally recognised as the one with which the *Titanic* collided. On the left in the photograph is another more distant iceberg.

The photo is informative for several reasons. Chunks of field ice litter the surface of the sea as far as the eye can see, confirming that Captain Smith drove straight into the ice field. There is a slight haze on the horizon. The iceberg, which has two peaks, appears substantially white in the daylight. Crucially, on either side of the iceberg and in front of it are lighter areas, which are almost certainly ledges, one of which *Titanic* grounded upon. As these ledges project above the surface of the water, had it been daylight when *Titanic* struck, then they would have been clearly visible. However, it was pitch dark and none of the eyewitnesses remarked on seeing such ledges.

What became of Bernice? On 14 July 1920 she married Bradford Hale Ellis a US born broker and Harvard graduate from Ohio. The couple settled in Los Angeles where their daughter Cara was born in 1922. Bernice was widowed in 1932. She never remarried. In 1986 she donated her Kodak camera and historic '*Titanic*' photographs to the Smithsonian Institution, a group of US museums and education and research centres. Bernice died in Los Angeles, California, on 11 February 1989 aged 96 years.

An Eminently Avoidable Accident: The Assumption that *Titanic* was Unsinkable

The myth of the unsinkable ship
In 1911 the White Star Line produced a publicity leaflet showing the two sister ships *Olympic* and *Titanic* and an artist's impression of how they would look when they were completed. In the final paragraph 'came the fatal phrase, 'as far as it's possible to do so these two wonderful vessels are designed to be unsinkable'.'[1] Captain Smith was clearly of the same opinion because shortly before assuming command of *Titanic*, he told his friends Mr and Mrs W. P. Willis of Flushing, Queens, New York City, that even if the ship received serious damage, she could still make it to port.[2]

When in darkness or in fog, hove to!
Referring to the four months in 1925 when he was a member of the Ice Patrol, Shubow declared that at night and in fog, the cutter on which he was sailing was obliged to have to, thus 'avoiding collision with any working ice by the aid of the powerful searchlights playing on the water periodically'.[3]

This statement raises two important points. Firstly, in the presence of ice, it behoves a ship to stop for fear of collision. Secondly, searchlights are an invaluable asset when ice is in the vicinity. Unfortunately, *Titanic* was equipped with no such searchlights.

In respect of the so-called 'accident', an angry Mrs J. Stuart White did not hold back. 'It was a careless, reckless thing. It seems almost useless to speak of it', she said, in an undoubted reference to the behaviour of Captain Smith. 'Just to think that on a beautiful starlit night – you could see the stars reflected in the water – with all those Marconi warnings, that they would allow such an accident to happen, with such a terrible loss of life and property. It is simply unbearable, I think.'[4]

40

The Debt Owed to Guglielmo Marconi

An Italian's vital role in the effecting of the rescue of those passengers and crew of the *Titanic* who survived, should not be overlooked. In fact, had it not been for him, every single soul aboard that ship would have perished. His name was Guglielmo Marconi, and he was 37 years old at the time of the *Titanic* disaster.

Guglielmo Giovanni Maria Marconi was born on 25 April 1874 in Bologna, Italy, to father Guiseppe, aristocrat and landowner, and mother, Annie (née Jameson) of the eponymous Irish family of whisky distillers.

He was educated first by private tutors and subsequently at the Istituto Cavallero in Florence, at Bologna University under Professor of Physics Augusto Righi, and at Livorno under Physics Professor Giotto Bizzarrini (At the latter place, he was also taught privately by Physics Professor Vincenzo Rosa of the Liceo Nicolini). In Righi's laboratory, Marconi acquired a knowledge of oscillators (transmitters) and resonators (receivers), as used by German physicist Heinrich Hertz. In 1887, Hertz became the first to give a satisfactory demonstration of the existence of 'Hertzian' waves – now known as radio waves – and also to demonstrate how they could be both transmitted and detected. However, as yet, no one had managed to transmit a signal a distance of more than about 100 yds). It fell to the youthful Marconi to achieve this breakthrough, which he did, using a raised aerial, and earthing both his transmitter and receiver.

Marconi conducted his first experiments in the granary at his home, Villa Griffone, Pontecchio, near Bologna, which he converted into a laboratory. His aim was to create a practical system of wireless telegraphy (i.e. one which did not depend on connecting wires, such as were used in the electric telegraph). In the spring of 1895, he succeeded in transmitting signals from his garden to a barn a mile or so away, even though the barn was hidden behind a hill.

Having had his proposals for a system of wireless communication rejected by the Ministry of Posts and Telegraphy in Rome, the twenty-two-year-old Marconi travelled to England, arriving in London with his apparatus on 2 February 1896. Having attracted the interest and support of William Preece, Chief Engineer to the British Post Office, he continued with his experiments, both in the capital and on Salisbury Plain, Wiltshire (in the presence of experts from the British Army and Navy). On 2 June 1896, he was granted the first British patent for wireless telegraphy.

On 13 May 1897, Marconi sent the first ever wireless signal across the open sea – a distance of nine miles across the Bristol Channel. In that summer, he returned to his home country where, at La Spezia on the coast of north-west Italy, he demonstrated his work to the Italian Navy. However, even now he failed to gain the support of the Italian government.

On 20 July 1897, Marconi established the Wireless Telegraph and Signal Company. In the summer of 1898, he transmitted messages from Osborne House – Queen Victoria's royal residence on the Isle of Wight – to the royal yacht *Osborne*. On 27 March 1899 he sent the first message (in Morse code) across the English Channel from South Foreland, St Margaret's Bay, Dover, Kent, to Wimereux, a coastal town near Boulogne. In the same year in the USA, he transmitted reports of the America's Cup yacht races from the liner *Ponce* to the mainland and proceeded to establish a wireless telegraphy company in America, just as he had done in Britain.

In November 1897, Marconi set up a wireless transmitting station on the cliffs at Alum Bay on the Isle of Wight. Four months later he established a second station at the Madeira Hotel, near Bournemouth Pier. Here, in the front garden, he erected an aerial and set up a laboratory in an underground cellar. Subsequently, having fallen out with the management of the hotel (whose proprietress is a Mrs Jolliffe), he moved his equipment to the house next door, 'Sandhills', in the garden of which he erected a 125ft-high mast in order to exchange messages with his Isle Wight station and with ships at sea.

In a letter to the Bournemouth *Daily Echo*, dated 4 May 1940, F.A. Olding of Moordown stated that he could 'well remember the day on which the 2-way communication was made, since I was privileged to see something of the delight with which the inventor declared his triumph on that occasion. On a warm, sunny afternoon, early in the season I think, I walked up the Bournemouth Pier with a message from my mother to her cousin, Capt. Cox of the SS *Victoria*, just as that vessel was berthing.

'I was startled to see a slight, dark man in a blue suit, dash excitedly up the gangway, waving his right hand to the pier master on the upper deck and shouting, "I've done it – I've done it".

Marconi was holding 'a small black box under his arm', and this enabled him that day both to send and to receive 'wireless' messages, for the very first time.

In 1900, Marconi changed the name of his enterprise to the 'Marconi Wireless Telegraph Company'. In September 1898, 'he transferred his headquarters to The Haven Hotel (formerly the Haven Coaching Inn), Sandbanks, Poole, where he again built a laboratory and erected an aerial'.

'The sending by Marconi on 12 December 1901 of the first transatlantic message, from Poldhu, Cornwall to Signal Hill, St John's, Newfoundland, a distance of over 2,000 miles, was the crowning moment of his career. This was despite the fact that scientists believed that wireless signals would be lost after 165 miles, due to the curvature of the Earth. He was then aged only twenty-seven.

In March 1905, Marconi married Beatrice, daughter of Irishman Edward Donough O'Brien, 14th Baron Inchiquin. In 1909 he was awarded the Nobel Prize for Physics sharing it with German physicist Karl Ferdinand Braun, inventor of the cathode ray oscillator.

Marconi and the UK and US Inquiries

At both the UK and the US Inquiries, Marconi spoke with the dignity and competence expected of a brilliant man to whom the world and in particular and the survivors of *Titanic* owed so much.

At the UK inquiry Marconi described how the first ship to be fitted with wireless telegraphy apparatus was the *Kaiser Wilhelm der Gross* of the North German Lloyd Company in the year 1900.[1]

At the US inquiry Marconi described himself as Electrical Engineer and Chairman of the British Marconi Company. Was the operator of Marconi wireless equipment on a ship responsible to his company, he was asked. 'He is responsible in so far as the commercial work goes – as to accounting for messages and the general conduction of a commercial telegraphic service', Marconi replied. However, in regard 'to his hours of labor and his general work in that capacity aboard ship', he would receive his orders from the captain.

How many wireless operators would a ship normally carry? If it was 'a large ship like the *Titanic*, the *Olympic*, the *Mauretania*, or the *Lusitania*', Marconi replied, 'they always carry two operators, but the smaller ships of the class or size of the *Carpathia* carry one'. By 'large', this was in respect of the 'average number of passengers carried'.

How powerful was the Marconi telegraph apparatus carried by *Titanic*, and by *Carpathia* which came to the rescue of her survivors? 'The wireless equipment on *Titanic*', said Marconi, 'was a fairly powerful set, capable, I should say, of communicating 400 or 500 miles during the daytime and much further during the night-time'. Carpathia, he Marconi, could 'transmit messages, under favourable circumstances, up to about 180 or 200 miles'. Since 1910, said Marconi, all passenger-carrying ships were obliged by law to carry wireless telegraph apparatus.[2]

Finally, said Marconi, 'I was exceedingly surprised and shocked' at the news 'that the *Titanic* had sunk with a very heavy loss of life. It seemed to me almost impossible'.[3]

41

The 1997 Dive on *Titanic*

The wreckage of *Titanic* lies at a depth of about 12,500 feet at Latitude 41° 726931' N and Longitude 49° 948253' W. It is in three main sections, separated by about half a mile: the stern (which has been severely crushed by the water pressure); a mid-section about 60 feet in length; the stern (which is upright and largely intact because, as it was full of water when the ship sank, it did not succumb to the deep-water pressure).

In August 1996 a team of scientists and engineers from the French Research Institute FREMER (Institut Français de Recherche pour L'Exploitation de la Mer) dived down to the *Titanic*, the wreckage of which was discovered in 1985, and examined the hull, including that section of it which was submerged in sediment. Leader of the expedition was Paul K. Matthias, President of Polaris Imaging, Inc, of Narragansett, Rhode Island, USA, who operated from the French mother ship *Ocean Voyager*, accompanied by the French vessel *Nadir*.

Prior to the *Titanic* expedition, Matthias carefully and thoroughly tested his techniques and equipment in the Mediterranean Sea off the coast of Greece. This was not the case in a subsequent expedition of 2023, which ended tragically as will be seen.

From the surface vessel the submersible *Nautile* was launched, for a 1½ hour freefall which took it to the ocean floor. *Nautile* contained three divers, one of whom was Matthias, and a laboratory, and the exploratory dive lasted for nine hours. With the aid of searchlights to penetrate the pitch darkness, *Titanic*'s hull was quickly located.

The hull lies in 50 feet or so or sediment, and the question was, was there damage to that section of the hull which was thus hidden from view? The answer was yes.

The team used a sonar device (sub-bottom profiler) to penetrate the sediment by sending and receiving acoustic signals in order to produce a seismic profile. In the 1997 documentary film '*Titanic*: Anatomy of a Disaster',

Matthias drew the positions of the punctures and splits on a diagram from the bow sternwards as follows:

Forepeak: one small puncture.
No. 1 Hold: two small punctures.
Straddling No. 1 Hold and No. 2 Hold across the intervening bulkhead: a 15-foot split.
Straddling No. 2 Hold and No. 3 Hold across the intervening bulkhead: a 32-foot split.
Straddling No. 6 Boiler Room and No. 5 Boiler Room: across the intervening bulkhead: a 36-foot split.

Therefore, in all, six compartments were flooded.

All the damage was on the starboard side, below the waterline but above the level of the double bottom. All the splits were about the thickness of a human adult finger, and the total area of splits and punctures totalled only about 12 square feet.

The splits in the hull 'appear to follow the hull plate', said Matthias. In other words, the hull plates had become separated at these points, indicating that the rivets had failed.[1]

The three major splits occurred at about 10 feet below the waterline, where the seawater pressure would have been 4.4 pounds per square inch initially, but once the bow section began to fill with water and the bows began to sink, the pressure would have increased dramatically, as would the quantity of water taken on board. For example, by midnight on 14/15 April an estimated 1,000 tons of water, and after another hour an estimated 25,000 tons.

Conclusion

The information gleaned from the 1996 Institut FREMER expedition, in respect of the damage to *Titanic*'s hull caused by her collision with the iceberg, was invaluable because it provides for a deeper understanding of the precise events of that fateful night, 14/15 April 1912.

The fact that it was the forepeak of *Titanic*'s bow which impacted with the iceberg, rather than it being a head-on collision, indicated that the ship had begun to turn to port in order (unsuccessfully) to avoid it.

Also, the fact that all the damage to *Titanic*'s hull occurred at about ten feet below the waterline indicates that the vessel struck a submarine protuberance (or ledge), which was also of necessity just below the waterline. That this ledge was a narrow one is deduced from the fact that simultaneously, the upper bow struck the upper part of the iceberg, causing ice to shower down only her deck.

So, we have *Titanic* travelling at almost her maximum speed straight at the iceberg, all her momentum (i.e. her mass times her velocity) being in a forward direction.

At the last minute, the ship made an abrupt turn to port, and began to turn in an anticlockwise direction, rotating about its pivot point, which was in in the midline and about one quarter of the way back from the bow, but too late. Almost immediately, the forepeak on the starboard side made violent contact with the iceberg, puncturing it in two places (below the waterline, but above the level of the double bottom). Furthermore, the impact would have increased the anticlockwise rotation of the ship.

In consequence, *Titanic*'s bow literally wrapped itself around the offending ledge, bouncing on and off it as the forward momentum of the ship was gradually dissipated. (Throughout this time, because the ship had scarcely begun to get under way on its new course, virtually all the momentum was still in the original forward direction.)

Evidently, as the bows of *Titanic* rotated anticlockwise around the ledge, areas of the hull corresponding to the various compartments within were successively punctured: the Forepeak (puncture); No. 1 Hold (puncture); Nos. 1 and 2 Holds (split); Nos. 2 and 3 Holds (split); Nos. 6 and 5 Boiler Rooms (split).

Because of the speed at which *Titanic* was travelling, the impact occurred with enormous violence. The force of the impact served to dissipate *Titanic*'s forward momentum, the energy being expended in puncturing, buckling, and splitting her steel plates. This all happened in the space of a few seconds, until she came to a virtual standstill. The ship was now doomed, there was no way the ship's pumps could have dealt with such a scenario, and nothing could be done to save her.

The prescience of Edward Wilding

36-year-old Edward Wilding was a member of the team of naval architects who designed *Titanic*. He was also a passenger aboard the ship.

On Day 19 of the UK Inquiry, Wilding referred to the puncturing of *Titanic*'s hull by the iceberg. Said he, 'I cannot believe that the wound was absolutely continuous the whole way. I believe that it was in a series of steps', and 'that before the ship finally cleared the iceberg as the helm was put over, she would be tending to swing her side into the iceberg, and that a very light contact was made in No. 4 [Boiler Room]. It seemed very probable ... that after the ship had finished tearing herself at the forward end of No. 5 [Boiler Room], she would tend to push herself against the iceberg a little, or push herself up the iceberg, and there would be a certain tendency, as the stern came round to aft under the helm, to bang against the iceberg again further aft'.

Had Wilding 'made any calculation as to the volume of water that came in through the apertures of this vessel?'. 'Assuming the forepeak and Nos. 1, 2 and 3 holds and No. 6 Boiler Room [had] flooded' this 'would mean that about 16,000 tons of water had found their way into the vessel', and the time taken for this would have been 'about 40 minutes'. [In fact, it is now known that the first six compartments were flooded.]

Wilding also estimated that 'the total area through which water was entering the ship, was somewhere about 12 square feet' and that 'the average width of the hole extending the whole way is only about three-quarters of an inch'.[2] This was the same conclusion that the FREMER research team came to 84 years later!

Wilding's calculations were widely disbelieved at the time. It is now recognized that he was not far from the mark!

42

Captain Smith: A Classic and Tragic Case of 'Hubris Syndrome'

Captain Smith was a remarkable man in that, from humble beginnings, he had become the White Star Line's go to man when it came to captaining its liners on their maiden voyages. He also had the gift of endearing himself to his passengers, in particular the first class ones, gaining their trust and confidence with his affability. However, there was a downside to his personality, as will be seen.

The myth of the unsinkable ship

In May 1907, after he had captained the *Adriatic* on her maiden voyage, Captain Smith told reporters in New York, 'that absolute disaster, involving the passengers, is inconceivable. Whatever happens, there will be time enough before the vessel sinks to save the life of every person on board. I will go a bit further. I can say that I cannot imagine any condition that would cause the vessel to founder. Modern shipbuilding has gone beyond that'.[1]

Said *Titanic* survivor Eva Hart, 'I entirely agree with my dear doctor Ballard's words. He said that the whole thing was a tribute to men's arrogance, and I agree with that. That man can be so arrogant as to build something and then claim it is unsinkable is the most arrogant thing to say.[2]

This was a reference to US Professor of Oceanography and explorer Robert Ballard, who discovered the wreck of the *Titanic* on 1 September 1985. But was this a true reflection of Ballard's views? The answer is yes.

Smith's supreme confidence as Captain

Captain Smith was quite blasé when he minimised the difference between his successive captaincies of ever larger vessels. In May 1907 he told reporters in New York, 'one might think that a captain taken from a small ship and put on a big one might feel the transition. Not at all. The skippers of the big vessels have grown up to them, year after year, through all these years.

First there was the sailing vessel and then what we now call small ships – they were big in the days gone by – and finally the giants of today'.[3] The various collisions and groundings in which Captain Smith had previously been involved belie his words!

How Captain Smith's officers, crew, and first class passengers eulogized him!

Second Officer Lightoller spoke admiringly of how his captain docked his ship at speed.

Steward Samuel Rule, who had served under Captain Smith 'on numerous ships starting back when the skipper had been a junior officer, later said of him, 'a better man never walked a deck. His crew knew him to be a good kind-hearted man, and we looked upon him as a sort of father'.'[4]

Author Kate Douglas-Wiggin spoke in glowing terms of Captain Smith, whom she had known 'from the time of the old *Britannic* until the day of his death'. She had 'crossed the ocean with Captain Smith twenty times or more', which she said was her 'pleasure and privilege. A kind of steady loyalty, to his profession, his duty, his friends, and his own ideal, always seemed to me the compass by which his life was set'.[5]

Captain Smith in a nutshell

The conclusions arrived at by the US Senate Investigation Committee were comprehensively damning:

> 'The ice positions so definitely reported to the *Titanic* just preceding the accident located ice on both sides of the track or lane which the *Titanic* was following, and in her immediate vicinity. No general discussion took place among the officers; no conference was called to consider these warnings; no heed was given to them. The speed was not relaxed, the lookout was not increased, and the only vigilance displayed by the officer of the watch was by instructions to the lookouts to keep 'a sharp lookout for ice'.[6]

What possible explanation can there be for Captain Smith's behaviour and actions?

Hubris is defined as excessive pride of self-confidence. In Greek tragedy it is defined as excessive pride towards or defiance of the gods, leading to nemesis.

Captain Smith: A Classic and Tragic Case of 'Hubris Syndrome'

Nemesis is defined as the inescapable agent of something's downfall.[7] Captain Smith may therefore be correctly described as *Titanic*'s nemesis.

Hubris in detail

The subject of 'Hubris' was elaborated upon in March 2009 in an article by Dr David Owen of the UK's House of Lords and UK psychiatrist Professor Jonathan Davidson, entitled, 'Hubris Syndrome: An Acquired Personality Disorder? A Study of US Presidents and UK Prime Ministers Over the Last 100 years'. Successful leadership, said the authors, was associated with 'charisma, charm, the ability to inspire, persuasiveness, breadth of vision, willingness to take risks, grandiose [extravagant or pretentious] aspirations, and bold self-confidence'. However, 'there is another side to this profile, for these very same qualities can be marked by impetuosity, a refusal to listen to or take advice, and a particular form of incompetence when impulsivity, recklessness and frequent inattention to detail predominate. This can result in disastrous leadership and cause damage on a large scale'.

Unlike other mental illnesses and personality disorders, hubris is reversible, in that it disappears when the power which the subject has hitherto exhibited fades. In other words, hubris is 'an acquired condition'.

An interesting feature of hubris is that the syndrome disappears as soon as the subject become separated from the hubristic environment. In the case of Captain Smith, this would have occurred at the very moment he heard that *Titanic* had struck the iceberg, was flooding rapidly, and about to sink. His power and prestige would suddenly have drained away, leaving him a lonely, desolate, and forlorn figure. His chief concern now would be to do everything he could to rectify the situation which, in his heart, he knew he had created.

The 'key concept', the authors continued, 'is that hubris syndrome is a disorder of the possession of power, particularly power which has been associated with overwhelming success, held for a period of years and with minimal constraint on the leader'. The syndrome only develops 'after power has been held for a period of time'.

The criteria necessary for the diagnosis of hubris syndrome to be made in an individual are as follows:

'A narcissistic propensity to see their world primarily as an arena in which to exercise power and seek glory.

A predisposition to take actions which seem likely to cast the individual in a good light – i.e. in order to enhance image, a disproportionate concern with image and presentation.

A messianic manner of talking about current activities and a tendency to exaltation; an identification with the nation, or organization to the extent that the individual regards his/her outlook and interests as identical; a tendency to speak in the third person or use the royal 'we'.

Excessive confidence in the individual's own judgement and contempt for the advice or criticism of others.

Exaggerated self-belief, bordering on a sense of omnipotence, in what they personally can achieve.

A belief that rather than being accountable to the mundane court of colleagues or public opinion, the court to which they answer is History or God.

An unshakable belief that in that court they will be vindicated.

Loss of contact with reality, often associated with progressive isolation, restlessness, recklessness, and impulsiveness.

A tendency to allow their 'broad vision', about the moral rectitude of a proposed course, to obviate the need to consider practicality, cost or outcomes.

Hubristic incompetence, where things go wrong because too much self-confidence has led the leader not to worry about the nuts and bolts of policy.'[8]

Clearly, for a ship's captain who is prone to hubris, a ship at sea provides the ideal environment in which this syndrome may develop. As a snowball accumulates snow and grows to a larger and larger size as it rolls down a snowy bank, so Captain Smith's hubris similarly grew and grew until finally he had complete confidence in himself and in his ship, which he regarded as unsinkable. Herein lay the seeds of destruction, of both *Titanic*, himself, and 1,496 passengers and crew.

Finally, a thought should be spared not only for those who died, and for their bereaved relatives, but also for those who laboured long and hard for over two years in the shipyard of Harland & Wolff to build *Titanic*. What their thoughts must have been when they learned the great ship had sunk on her maiden voyage, and that all their efforts had been to no avail, can only be imagined.

Appendix

Provisions

Titanic carried 6,611 tons of coal.

Titanic carried the following provisions:

Condensed milk 600 gallons
Ice cream 1,750 quarts
Shelled walnuts 411 cases
Flour 250 barrels
Towels 25,000
Edison gramophones 1 case
Cameras and stands 3 cases
Oyster forks 1,000
Fresh fish 11,000 pounds
Grape scissors (to cut the stems of bunches of grapes) 100
Cutlery 44,000 pieces
Musical instruments 5 cases
Opium (for medicinal use, to relieve pain and for surgical anaesthesia) 4 cases
Asparagus tongs (to handle asparagus spears without them breaking) 400
Asparagus 800 bundles
Coal 5,900 tons
Celery glasses 300
Crockery 57,600 pieces
Grandfather clocks 2 cases
Sugar 10,000 pounds
Glassware 29,000 pieces
Anchovies 75 cases
Scientific instruments 1 case
Eggs 40,000
Raw feathers 8 cases
Grapefruit 50 boxes
Oranges 3,600
Calabashes (any of various gourds: large, fleshy, edible fruit) 16 cases
Rabbit hair (used in the manufacture of hats and coats) 1 case
Horsehair (used for upholstery, brushes, and the bows of musical instruments) 2 cases
Straw hats 4 cases

Notes

British Wreck Commissioners Inquiry is abbreviated to UK Day 1, etc.
United States Senate Inquiry is abbreviated to US Day 1, etc.

Chapter 1: *Titanic*: The World's Largest Movable Object: The White Star Line
1. 'White Star Line', *Wikipedia*.
2. Scarth, Alan, *Titanic and Liverpool*.
3. Blake, John, *The Titanic Pocket Book: A Passenger's Guide*, p.16.
4. McCluskie, Tom, *Anatomy of the Titanic*, p.13.
5. Soanes, Catherine and Angus Stevenson (editors), *Oxford Dictionary of English*.

Chapter 2: *Titanic*: A Further Description
1. UK Day 19.
2. McCluskie, Tom, *Anatomy of the Titanic*, p.94.
3. Blake, John, *The Titanic Pocket Book: A Passenger's Guide*, p.37.
4. Halpern, Samuel, '*Titanic*'s Hidden Deck', *Encyclopedia Titanica*, 2004.
5. McCluskie, Tom, op. cit., p.26.
6. Soanes, Catherine and Angus Stevenson (editors), *Oxford Dictionary of English*. OED
7. Ibid.
8. Ibid.

Chapter 3: *Titanic*'s Decks
1. Blake, John, *The Titanic Pocket Book: A Passenger's Guide*, p.91.
2. Ibid, p.41.

Chapter 4: Lifeboats and Safety Equipment
1. Blake, John, *The Titanic Pocket Book: A Passenger's Guide*, pp.119–120.
2. Ibid, pp.44–5.
3. US Day 8.

Chapter 5: First Class Luxury!
1. Blake, John, *The Titanic Pocket Book: A Passenger's Guide*, p.59
2. McCluskie, Tom, *Anatomy of the Titanic*, p.116.

Chapter 6: *Titanic* Sets Sail
1. Newbery, Maria, *SeaCity Museum: The Lives; The Times*, p.8.
2. Time references are derived from '*Titanic* – A Maiden Voyage Timeline', atlanticliners.com, online.
3. Newbery, Maria, op. cit., p.9.
4. Soanes, Catherine and Angus Stevenson (editors), *Oxford Dictionary of English*.

Chapter 7: *Titanic*'s Captain, Edward Smith
1. Captain Edward J. Smith, Service Records, National Maritime Museum, London.

Chapter 8: Captain Smith: Bravado: Previous Mishaps
1. Cooper, Gary J., *Titanic Captain: The Life of Edward John Smith*, pp.120–1.
2. Ibid, p.72.
3. Ibid, p.105.
4. Ibid, p.131.
5. Ibid, pp.90–1.
6. *Captain E. J. Smith Memorial: A Souvenir of July 29th 1914*, pp.30–31, in Cooper, pp.80–1.
7. Lightoller, Charles Herbert, *Titanic and Other Ships*, p.164.

Chapter 9: *Titanic*'s Officers
1. 'Henry Tingle Wilde', *Wikipedia*.
2. 'William McMaster Murdoch', *Wikipedia*.
3. UK Inquiry.
4. UK Inquiry.
5. UK Inquiry.
6. UK Inquiry.
7. 'James Paul Moody, *Wikipedia*.

Chapter 10: *Titanic*'s Crew
1. Information about the crew derived from 'Crew of the *Titanic*', *Wikipedia*.
2. Blake, John, *The Titanic Pocket Book: A Passenger's Guide*, p.90.
3. 'Mabel Kate Bennett', RMS *Titanic* Stewardess, *Encyclopedia Titanica* online.
4. SeaCity Museum.
5. Blake, John, op. cit., pp.87–8.

Chapter 11: *Titanic*'s Passengers
1. Blake, John, *The Titanic Pocket Book: A Passenger's Guide*, p.54.
2. Ibid, p.54.
3. Ibid, p.111.
4. Ibid, p.101.
5. Ibid, p.103.

Chapter 12: Safety: The Board of Trade Passenger Certificate: Failure to Perform a Lifeboat Drill
1. Maiden Voyage Timeline MVT
2. Maiden Voyage Timeline MVT
3. UK Day 21.
4. US Day 1.
5. US Day 4.
6. UK Day 21.
7. UK Day 19
8. US Day 7.
9. US Day 7.

Chapter 13: The Atlantic Ocean Beckons: 'Tracks'
1. Blake, John, *The Titanic Pocket Book: A Passenger's Guide*, p.114.
2. Soanes, Catherine and Angus Stevenson (editors), *Oxford Dictionary of English*.
3. US Day 4
4. US Day 5.
5. Halpern, Samuel W., 'Mistakes in the Night', online.
6. US Day 4.
7. US Day 5.
8. US Day 4
9. US Day 4.
10. US Day 4.
11. US Day 5.
12. US Day 5.

Chapter 14: The Weather and Sea Conditions up to the Night of 14/15 April 1912
1. US Day 1.
2. US Day 5.
3. US Day 1.
4. US Day 7.
5. US Day 1.
6. UK Day 13.
7. US Day 4.
8. US Day 7.
9. US Day 7.
10. Soanes, Catherine and Angus Stevenson (editors), *Oxford Dictionary of English*.
11. Ibid.
12. UK Day 4.
13. UK Day 15
14. Soanes, Catherine and Angus Stevenson (editors), op. cit.
15. 'Bells, Clocks, Watches Schedules and Time Adjustments', Titanicology.com/WatchTablesFile online
16. Andrews, Samantha, 'Lifting the Fog ... or is that Mist?', Ocean Oculus, online.

Chapter 15: Sunday 14 April 1912: Captain Smith's Instructions to his Officers and Their Instructions to *Titanic*'s Lookouts: What They Saw
1. US Day 5.
2. US Day 4.
3. US Day 7.
4. US Day 3.
5. US Day 1.
6. McCluskie, Tom, *Anatomy of the Titanic*, p.97.

Chapter 16: *Titanic*'s Lookouts; Their Previous Experience and Capabilities
1. '*Titanic* Pages', *Titanic* History Website, and *Encyclopedia Titanica* online.
2. US Day 7.
3. US Day 7.
4. UK Day 15.

Chapter 17: The Mystery of the Missing Binoculars
1. UK Day 15.
2. UK Day 4.
3. UK Day 4.
4. US Day 7.
5. UK Day 10.
6. US Day 4.
7. UK Day 15.
8. UK Day 10.
9. US Day 7.
10. US Day 7.

Chapter 18: Warnings of Ice and Icebergs, Some of Which Did Not Reach the Bridge, and All of Which Captain Smith Chose to Ignore
1. Times given are as stated in '*Titanic* – A Maiden Voyage Timeline', online.
2. US Day 3.
3. US Day 3.

Chapter 19: Aboard *Titanic*, was there any Inkling of Ice of Icebergs in the Vicinity?
1. US Day 3.
2. US Day 7.
3. US Day 5.
4. US Day 12.
5. US Day 8.

Chapter 20: Who was On Watch on that Fateful Night of 14/15 April 1912? First Sight of the Iceberg
1. US Day 1.
2. US Day 4.
3. US Day 4.
4. US Day 5.
5. US Day 4.
6. US Day 4.
7. UK Day 15.
8. US Day 4.
9. UK Day 15.
10. UK Day 4.
11. US Day 4.
12. US Day 5.
13. US Day 5.
14. UK Day 4.

Chapter 21: The Collision: The Fatal Turn to Port
1. US Day 10.
2. US Day 4.
3. US Day 4.
4. US Day 5.
5. US Day 5.

6. US Day 4.
7. US Day 7.
8. US Day 7.
9. US Day 7.
10. US Day 7.
11. US Day 7.
12. US Day 9.
13. US Day 10.
14. US Day 13.
15. US Day 13.
16. Mahala Douglas, Affidavit, US Day 15.
17. US Day 7.
18. US Day 3.
19. US Day 5.
20. UK Day 4.
21. US Day 4.
22. US Day 5.
23. US Day 7.
24. US Day 4.
25. US Day 15.
26. US Day 3.
27. US Day 4.
28. UK Day 4.
29. US Day 4.
30. UK Day 4.
31. US Day 5.
32. US Day 7.
33. US Day 4.
34. US Day 3.
35. US Day 3.
36. US Day 7.
37. US Day 11.
38. US Day 7.
39. US Day 13.
40. US Day 13.
41. US Day 9.
42. US Day 7.
43. Kuntz, Tom, *The Titanic Disaster Hearings*, p.543.
44. US Day 4.
45. Shubow, Leo, *Iceberg Dead Ahead*, p.125.
46. US Day 4.
47. UK Day 19.
48. US Day 5.
49. UK Day 4.
50. US Day 7.
51. US Day 7.
52. US Day 7.

Chapter 22: The Outcome of the Impact
1. US Day 7.
2. US Day 7.
3. Soanes, Catherine and Angus Stevenson (editors), *Oxford Dictionary of English*.
4. Halpern, Samuel, 'Finding the Apparent Flotation Pivot Point', online.

Chapter 23: Survival! The Inadequately Filled Lifeboats
1. Halpern, Samuel, *Report into the Loss of SS Titanic*, pp.47,67.
2. Lightoller p.177.
3. 'British Wreck Commissioner's Inquiry Report', Board of Trade's Administration, *Titanic* Inquiry Project online.
4. Halpern, Samuel, op. cit., p.135.
5. Ibid, p.143.
6. Lightoller p.179.
7. US Day 12
8. US Day 7.

Chapter 24: The Ice Field into which *Titanic* had Sailed
1. US Day 4.
2. US Day 3.
3. US Day 3.
4. US Day 5.
5. US Day 5.
6. US Day 6.
7. US Day 7.
8. US Day 7.
9. US Day 7.
10. US Day 7.
12. US Day 10.
13. US Day 11.
14. US Day 11.
15. US Day 12.
16. US Day 7.
17. UK Day 21.
18. UK Day 21.
19. US Day 11.

Chapter 25: The Speed of *Titanic* on Impact with the Iceberg: Visibility at the Crucial Time: Time Available to React to the Presence of the Iceberg
1. Blake, John, *The Titanic Pocket Book: A Passenger's Guide*, p.5.
2. US Day 4.
3. US Day 4.
4. UK Day 4.
5. Halpern, Samuel, *Report into the Loss of SS Titanic*, p.74.
6. UK Day 4.
7. UK Day 15.
8. UK Day 4.
9. US Day 7.

168 Titanic

10. US Day 7.
11. US Day 7.
12. US Day 9.
13. US Day 13.
14. US Day 7.
15. US Day 7.
16. US Day 9.
17. US Day 7.
18. 'Why is Glacier Ice Blue?', Woods Hole Oceanographic Institution online.
19. 'Iceberg that struck the *Titanic*', *Wikipedia*. Halpern, Samuel. Account of the Ship's Journey across the Atlantic. In: Samuel Halpern (Hrsg.): Report into the Loss of the SS *Titanic*: A Centennial Reappraisal. *The History Press*, Stroud 2016 (2012), p.85.
20. Shubow, Leo, *Iceberg Dead Ahead*, pp.176–7.
21. Randall A Rosenfeld, Astronomical Society of Canada, from M. Jean Vallieres, COELIX APEX 2.124.
22. Halpern, Samuel, op. cit., p.88.
23. Soanes, Catherine and Angus Stevenson (editors), *Oxford Dictionary of English*.
24. Ibid.
25. Halpern, Samuel, op. cit., pp.51–2.
26. 'Minimum Illumination: An Overview', *ScienceDirect Topics*, online.
27. Soanes, Catherine and Angus Stevenson (editors), op. cit.
28. Ibid.
29. Ibid.
30. Ibid.
31. 'Illuminance – Recommended Light Levels Working Activities and Light Levels – Required Illuminance', The Engineering ToolBox, online.
32. Soanes, Catherine and Angus Stevenson (editors), op. cit.

Chapter 26: The Origin of Icebergs: Were Icebergs a One-off Phenomenon in 1912, at the Location in the Atlantic Ocean where *Titanic* Sank?
1. 'Where do North Atlantic Icebergs Come From?', Infoplease, 9 September 2022, online.
2. Shubow, Leo, *Iceberg Dead Ahead*, pp.58–9.
3. US Day 3
4. Bigg, Grant R. and David J. Wilton, 'Iceberg Risk in the *Titanic* Year of 1912: Was It Exceptional?', Royal Meteorological Society, 10 April 2014 online.

Chapter 27: The Invidious Position of *Titanic*'s Lookouts: Absence of Searchlights; Absence of Binoculars; Absence of Goggles
1. US Day 5.
2. US Day 3.
3. '*Titanic*'s Navigation Lights', r/*Titanic*facts online.
4. UK Day 15.
5. US Day 4.
6. US Day 7.
7. US Day 7.
8. *Lookout Manual 1943*, Nav Pers 170069, Naval History and Heritage Command, online.

Chapter 28: Fate of the Captain, Passengers and Crew: Human Drama and Human Tragedy
1. US Day 10.
2. US Day 13.
3. US Day 13.
4. US Day 10.
5. US Day 10.
6. US Day 7.
7. US Day 7.
8. US Day 16.
9. US Day 7.
10. US Day 7.
11. US Day 11.
12. I am grateful to Jan Marsh for sharing with me her research into Jacob Pride.
13. 'Crew of the *Titanic*', *Wikipedia*.

Chapter 29: The Alleged Negligence of Captain Stanley Lord of the SS *Californian*
1. Kuntz, Tom, *The Titanic Disaster Hearings*, pp.545–6.
2. Gillespie, John G., 'When Is A Rocket Called A Distress Signal Or Just A Flash In The Sky?', *Titanic Historical Society*.
3. Ibid.
4. Lightoller, Charles Herbert, *Titanic and Other Ships*, pp.178–180.
5. British Inquiry, 'Circumstances in Connection with the SS *Californian*'. Gracie, pp. 8–9.
6. Kuntz, Tom, op. cit., p.547.
7. UK Inquiry, Report
8. Halpern, Samuel, *Report into the Loss of SS Titanic*, p.183.
9. Ibid, p.185.
10. Ibid, p.184.
11. Ibid, p.186.
12. Ibid, p.187.

Chapter 30: Captain Lord's Defence
1. UK Day 7
2. UK Inquiry
3. UK Day 7.
4. US Day 8.
5. US Day 8.
6. UK Day 7.
7. US Day 8.
8. UK Day 7.
9. US Day 8.
10. UK Day 7.
11. UK Day 7.
12. UK Day 7.
13. UK Day 7.
14. US Day 8.
15. UK Day 7.
16. UK Day 8.
17. US Day 8.
18. UK Day 7.

Chapter 32: Second Officer Lightoller's Account in More Detail
1. Lightoller, Charles Herbert, *Titanic and Other Ships*, p.170.
2. Ibid, pp.170–1.
3. US Day 4.
4. US Day 4.
5. Lightoller, Charles Herbert, op. cit., p.171.
6. Ibid, p.171.
7. Ibid, p.172
8. Ibid, p.172
9. Ibid, pp.172–3
10. Ibid, p.172
11. Ibid, pp.172–3.
12. Ibid, p.173
13. Ibid, p.174.
14. Ibid, p.175.
15. Ibid, p.176.
16. Ibid, p.177.
17. Ibid, p.178.
18. Ibid, p.173.

Chapter 33: Weaknesses in *Titanic*'s Design and Construction
1. Soanes, Catherine and Angus Stevenson (editors), *Oxford Dictionary of English*.
2. Ibid.
3. Newman, Michael E., 'NIST Reveals How Tiny Rivets Doomed a *Titanic* Vessel', NIST, 13 February 2019 online.
4. UK Day 20.
5. UK Day 20.
6. UK Day 19.

Chapter 34: Verdict of the UK and US Inquiries
1. Kuntz, Tom, *The Titanic Disaster Hearings*, pp.547–8.
2. Ibid, p.541.
3. Ibid, p.543.
4. UK Day 21.
5. Kuntz, Tom, op. cit., p.551.
6. UK Day 17.
7. British Wreck Commissioner's Enquiry: Report.

Chapter 35: J. Bruce Ismay's Testimony to the UK and US Inquiries
1. UK Day 16.
2. Ibid.
3. US Day 11.
4. UK Day 17.
5. UK Day 16.
6. UK Day 17.
7. UK Day 16.
8. UK Day 17.
9. UK Day 16.

10. UK Day 17.
11. Ibid.
12. UK Day 16.
13. Ibid.
14. Ibid.
15. US Day 1.
16. US Day 11.
17. US Day 11.
18. US Day 1.
19. US Day 11.
20. US Day 1.
21. US Day 11.
22. Ibid.
23. US Day 15.
24. US Day 11.
25. Ibid.
26. Ibid.
27. US Day 11.
28. US Day 1.
29. Ibid.

Chapter 36: Morgan Robertson's Prophetic Novella: *The Wreck of the Titan* Or, *Futility* (1898): What If?
1. Robertson, Morgan, The Wreck of the Titan, Or Futility, McClure's Magazine and Metropolitan Magazine, 1898.

Chapter 37: Eva Hart: A Survivor's Account
1. 'The Story of Captain Smith and the *Titanic*', Lion Heart Film Works, 1992.

Chapter 38: Bernice Palmer, Her Camera, and the Iceberg
1. San Bernardino Sun, 15 April 1982.

Chapter 39: An Eminently Avoidable Accident: The Assumption that *Titanic* was Unsinkable
1. Cooper, Gary J., *Titanic Captain: The Life of Edward John Smith*, p.137, ref. 1.
2. Ibid, p.157, ref. 22.
3. Shubow, Leo, *Iceberg Dead Ahead*, p.158.
4. US Day 12.

Chapter 40: The Debt Owed to Guglielmo Marconi
1. UK Day 26.
2. US Day 1.
3. US Day 6.

Chapter 41: The 1997 Dive on *Titanic*
1. '*Titanic*: Anatomy of Disaster', Discovery Channel, 1997.
2. UK Day 19.

Chapter 42: Captain Smith: A Classic and Tragic Case of 'Hubris Syndrome'
1. Cooper, Gary J., *Titanic Captain: The Life of Edward John Smith*, p.120.
2. 'The Story of Captain Smith and the *Titanic*', Lion Heart Film Works, 1992.
3. Cooper, Gary J., op. cit., p.119.
4. Ibid, p.80, ref. 26.
5. Ibid, pp.81–2, ref. 28.
6. Kuntz, Tom, *The Titanic Disaster Hearings*, p.541.
7. Soanes, Catherine and Angus Stevenson (editors), *Oxford Dictionary of English*.
8. Owen, David, and Jonathan Davidson, 'Hubris Syndrome: An Acquired Personality Disorder? A Study of US Presidents and UK Prime Ministers Over the Last 100 years', *Brain* 132 (Pt 5): pp.1396–1406, March 2009.

Bibliography

Blake, John, *The Titanic Pocket Book: A Passenger's Guide* (Osprey Publishing, Oxford, UK, 2018).
Cooper, Gary J., *Titanic Captain: The Life of Edward John Smith* (The History Press, Stroud, UK, 2011).
Halpern, Samuel, *Report into the Loss of SS Titanic* (The History Press, Stroud, UK, 2016).
Kuntz, Tom (editor), *The Titanic Disaster Hearings* (Pocket Books, London, New York, 1998).
Lightoller, Charles Herbert, *Titanic and Other Ships* (Lulu.com, 2010).
McCluskie, Tom, *Anatomy of the Titanic*, PRC Publishing, London, 1998.
Newbery, Maria, *SeaCity Museum: The Lives; The Times* (Jarrold Publishing, Peterborough, UK, 2014).
Scarth, Alan, *Titanic and Liverpool* (Liverpool University Press, New York, USA, 2010).
Shubow, Leo, *Iceberg Dead Ahead* (Bruce Humphries, Boston, 1959).
Soanes, Catherine and Angus Stevenson (editors), *Oxford Dictionary of English* (Oxford University Press, Oxford, New York, 2005).

Index

Adriatic 22, 24, 26, 29–30, 32, 51, 157
Agra 23
Amerika 59–60
Amoy 23
Andrews, Thomas 33, 37
Antillian 61, 110
Astor, John Jacob IV 39, 100
Astor, Mrs Madeleine T. (née Force) 100, 102
Athinai 60
Arzilla 23

Ballard, Robert 157
Baltic 22–24, 29, 60, 105, 133, 136
Barr, James Clayton 58–59, 111
Bartlett, George A. 41–42, , 86, 128–129
Beaumont, John C. H. 40
Bell, Joseph 34
Bennett, Mabel Kate (née Pilgrim) 35
Bigelow, Henry B. 95
Bigg, Grant R. 96
Bingham, John Charles, Lord Mersey 129
Birma 105
Blake, John 17
Bowyer, George 20
Boxhall, Joseph Groves 31–32, 46, 48–49, 58, 63–64, 69, 71–73, 84, 95–97, 106, 119, 122
Brailey, Theodore 38
Braun, Karl Ferdinand 151
Brice, Walter T. 70
Bricoux, Roger M. 38
Bride, Harold S. 37, 61, 120
Britannic 3, 23–24, 158
British Seafarers' Union 19
Buckley, Daniel 70, 100–101
Butt, Archibald 39

Canadian Pacific Railway 132, 135
Carlisle, Alexander M. 3

Caronia 58–59
Carpathia 82, 84–86, 103–105, 114–115, 117, 129–130, 137, 144–146, 152
Caussin, Charles-Fernand 57–58
Celtic. 22–24, 30
Chadburns Telegraph Company of Liverpool 15
Chalmers, Alfred 80–81
Chambers, Norman C. 70, 73
Chapman, Ethel (née Smith) 103
Chapman, Joseph 103
Cherbourg, France 4, 20
City of New York 20, 27
Clarke, Maurice 41
Collins, John 75, 101
Cooper, Gary J. 26
Coptic 23–24, 29
Coronian 111
Crawford, Alfred George 36, 90
Crowe George F., 42, 70, 83, 85
Cufic 24, 29

Daily Mirror 102
Daunt Rock 21
Davidson, Jonathan 159
Dent, Frederick 70
Douglas, Mahala (née Dutton) 71, 137
Douglas, Walter D. 71
Douglas-Wiggin, Kate 158

Etches, Henry S. 73
Evans, Alfred Frank 47, 49, 51, 55, 65, 102
Evans, Cyril F. 109, 111, 115, 117
Evans, Frank 102 ??

Fastnet Rock 43
Firemen's Union 19
Fleet, Frederick 47, 52–56, 65, 69, 72, 75, 89, 98
Foecke, Tim 125

Index

Frankfurt 105, 115
Futrelle, Jacques 39

Gatti, Gaspare A. P. 'Luigi' 37
Germanic 24, 26, 30–31
Gibson, Andrew 22
Gillespie, John G. 105–106
Goodwin, Augusta 102
Goodwin, Charles Edward 102
Goodwin, Frederick Joseph 102
Goodwin, Harold Victor 102
Goodwin, Jessie Allis Mary 102
Goodwin, Lilian Augusta 102
Goodwin, Sidney Leslie 102
Goodwin, William Frederick 102
Gordon, Cosmo E. Duff 39
Gracie, Archibald 103, 107–109
Guggenheim, Benjamin 25, 39

Haines, Albert 85
Halifax, Nova Scotia, 104
Halpern, Samuel 44, 77–78, 91–92, 109
Hancock, Joseph 22
Hanley, Staffordshire 22
Harder, Dorothy (née Annan) 70
Harder, George A. 70, 73
Harder, William 90
Hardy, John 73, 85
Harland & Wolff 3, 5–6, 25, 37, 126, 131, 160
Harland, Edward J. 3
Harper, Henry S. 39
Harris, Henry B. 39
Hart, Esther 143–144
Hart, Eva 143–145, 157
Hart, Benjamin 143–144
Hartley, Wallace Henry 37, 40
Hayes, Charles M. 39
Hichens, Robert 33, 44, 49, 63–65, 69, 84
Hogg, George Alfred 47, 51–52, 54–56, 63, 65, 98

International Mercantile Marine Company 4, 107, 110, 137
Irish Sea 19
Isaacs, Rufus 133
Ismay, Thomas 3
Ismay, Joseph Bruce 3–4, 131–138, 142

Jewell, Archie 34, 47, 52, 55, 65

Knuth, H. 59–60
Krins, George 38
Krol, Watze 59

Labrador Current 48, 86, 95, 119, 121
Labrador Sea 95
Laing, F. 126
La Touraine 21, 57–58
Lee, Paul 57
Lee, Reginald Robinson 47, 52, 54–55, 65–66, 71–72, 75, 88–89
Leslie, Lucy N. M. 39
Lightoller, Charles Herbert 28–32, 41, 46–47, 49, 55–56, 61, 64, 69, 71–72, 78, 80–82, 88, 97, 100, 106–107, 109, 118–119, 121–124, 142, 158
Lizzie Fennell 23
Lowe, Harold Godfrey 32, 41, 44–46, 48, 71, 81–84, 102, 119
Lord, Mabel Henrietta (née Tutton) 110
Lord, Stanley 16, 63, 90, 105–117, 130

Mackay-Bennett 104
Madge Wildfire 23
Majestic 24, 26–29, 31, 56, 80, 122
Marconi, Beatrice (nee O'Brien) 151
Marconi, Guglielmo Giovanni Maria 108, 149–152
Marconi Wireless Telegraph Company 15, 36–37, 151
Matthias, Paul K. 153–154
Maury, Matthew F. 141
McCarthey, Daniel 26
McCluskie, Thomas G. 6–7, 17, 50
Mesaba 61, 119–120
Meyer, Leila (née Saks) 137
Meyer, Edgar J. 137
Millet, Francis D. 39
Minia 104
Montmagny 104
Moody, James Paul 32, 42, 48–49, 64, 82, 100, 141
Moore, George 85–86, 101–102
Mount Temple 105, 109
Mullen, James 26

Murdoch, William McMaster 29–30, 32, 41, 46–47, 65–66, 71, 73, 82, 100–101, 119, 121–122

Nadir 153
Nantucket Light Vessel 43–44
National Sailors' Union 19
Newman, Michael E. 125
Newfoundland 48, 60, 95–96, 104, 151
New York Times 26
Nichols, Alfred W. S. 33
Noordam 59
Noorland 27

Oceanic 30–32, 34, 51–52, 54–56, 80, 98, 104, 122
Oceanic Steam Navigation Company 4
Ocean Voyager 153
Olliver, Alfred 70–73, 76, 89–90
O'Loughlin, Francis W. N. 133
Olympic 3–4, 22, 24–25, 29–30, 36, 42, 52, 86, 105, 125, 131, 148, 152
Osman, Frank 75, 89–90
Ottawa 104
Owen, David 159

Palmer, Bernice Gardner 146–147
Palmer, Florence Cleugh (née Brydon) 146
Palmer, Frederick Douglas 146
Perkins, Laurence A. 37
Phillips, John G. ('Jack') 37, 61–62, 120
Pilkington, John 3
Pirrie, Lord 3, 25, 37
Pitman, Herbert John 31, 41, 43–46, 48–49, 64, 69, 72–74, 82, 84, 88, 119

Quebec 23
Queenstown, southern Ireland 4, 20, 27, 56

Ranson, Joseph Barlow 60
Ratti, Giuseppe 99
Ray, Frederick Dent 70
Record 23
Republic 22–24, 26, 29
Robertson, Morgan 139
Roebling, Washington A 39
Royal Astronomical Society of Canada 91
Rostron, Arthur Henry 129–130
Royal Naval Reserve 20, 22, 51

Ryerson, Mrs Emily 102, 137
Ryerson, Ellen 102
Runic 24, 30

Scarth, Alan 4
Schwabe, Gustav Christian 3
Sedunary, Madge (née Tizzard) 103
Sedunary, Samuel Francis 104
Senator Weber 22–23
Shubow, Leo 74, 94–95, 148
Smith, Catherine (née Hancock) 22
Smith, Edward 22
Smith, (Sarah) Eleanor (née Pennington) 22
Smith, Edward John 9, 15, 20–31, 41, 49–50, 58–60, 62, 64–65, 73–74, 76, 81, 84, 86, 100, 116–117, 119, 123–124, 126, 128–130, 133–137, 140–143, 146, 148, 157–159
Smith, Helen Melville 22, 25
Smith, William Alden 128
Southampton Times 104
Stone, Herbert 112–114, 117
Stanley, Phillip 61
Steele, Benjamin 41
Steffanson, Mauritz B. 101
Stengel, C. E. Henry 73, 85–87
Stewart, George F. 113
St Louis 27
Straus, Isidor 39
Symons, George T. M. 46–47, 51–52, 55–56, 65, 70, 75

Thayer, Mrs Marian L. 102
Trinity House 20

Virginian 105, 115

Wreck of the Titan, The, or, Futility 139
Ward, William 73–74, 85
White, Ella Bertha Stuart (née Holmes) 63, 82
White, Mrs J. Stuart 86, 148
White, John Stuart 63
White Star Company 4, 25, 131, 135
White Star Line 3–4, 16, 19, 22–23, 25, 27, 29–32, 34, 37, 40–41, 44, 51–52, 54, 56, 104, 118, 124, 132, 137, 141, 148, 157
Widener, George D. 39

Wilde, Henry Tingle 29–30, 47, 64, 81–82, 100
Wilding, Edward 5, 42, 74, 78, 126–127, 156
Williams, J. E. Hodder 27
Willis, Mrs W. P. 148
Willis, W. P. 148
Wilson, Henry 3
Wilton, David J. 97
Wind and Current Charts: Gales in the Atlantic, 141

Wireless Telegraph and Signal Company 150
Wolff, Gustav Wilhelm 3
Woolner, Hugh 70, 85, 100–101

Young, Maria Grice 63

Zeusler, Fred 91

Dear Reader,

We hope you have enjoyed this book, but why not share your views on social media? You can also follow our pages to see more about our other products: facebook.com/penandswordbooks or follow us on X @penswordbooks

You can also view our products at www.pen-and-sword.co.uk (UK and ROW) or www.penandswordbooks.com (North America).

To keep up to date with our latest releases and online catalogues, please sign up to our newsletter at: www.pen-and-sword.co.uk/newsletter

If you would like a printed catalogue with our latest books, then please email: enquiries@pen-and-sword.co.uk or telephone: 01226 734555 (UK and ROW) or email: uspen-and-sword@casematepublishers.com or telephone: (610) 853-9131 (North America).

We respect your privacy and we will only use personal information to send you information about our products.

Thank you!